PRESS

C. A. PRESS

JENNI RIVERA
THE INCREDIBLE STORY OF A WARRIOR BUTTERFLY

Novelist, pianist and journalist, Leila Cobo is the Executive Director of Latin Content and Programming for *Billboard* magazine. Under her tenure, *Billboard* has expanded its coverage of Latin music to unprecedented levels, and now has a complete weekly section dedicated solely to Latin music. Leila also programs the yearly *Billboard Latin Music Conference*, the largest gathering of the Latin music industry in the United States.

Originally from Cali, Colombia, Leila won a Fulbright scholarship to attend graduate school and earn a Master's Degree in Communications from the Annenberg School of Communications at the University of Southern California, after having earned a Master's Degree for concert piano performance from the Manhattan School of Music in New York. She was the pop music critic for *The Miami Herald* and wrote about culture for *The Los Angeles Times*. Leila has written album notes for many top-selling artists including Shakira, Ricky Martin, Julio Iglesias and Chayanne. As a musical expert, she has been invited to serve as a judge for many competitions, including the Viña del Mar International Song Festival in Chile, and Objectivo Fama Internacional, in Mexico.

In addition to her position at *Billboard*, Leila is the Executive Producer and host of *Estudio Billboard*, the acclaimed television show where she has interviewed the greatest artists in Latin music, including Maná, Juan Luis Guerra, Jenni Rivera and Gloria Estefan.

Leila is a coauthor of the *Billboard Illustrated Encyclopedia of Music* and contributing writer for *Quinceañera*, an essay collection published by HarperCollins. As a fiction writer, her first novel, *Tell Me Something True*, was published in October 2009 to critical acclaim by Grand Central Publishing/Hachette. Her second novel, *The Second Time We Met*, was published in 2012.

In 2008, the Miami magazine *Ocean Drive* named her one of its "Power Brokers." She also won the Premio Orquídea, which honors exceptional Colombians living abroad, for her work as a journalist. Leila is considered a leading expert on Latin music, and is constantly referenced in music media. She lives in Miami, Florida. For more information, visit her Web site:

www.leilacobo.com

JENNI RIVERA

THE INCREDIBLE STORY OF
A WARRIOR BUTTERFLY

Leila Cobo

C. A. PRESS
Penguin Group (USA)

C. A. PRESS

Published by the Penguin Group
Penguin Group (USA) Inc., 375 Hudson Street,
New York, New York 10014, USA

USA | Canada | UK | Ireland | Australia | New Zealand | India | South Africa | China
Penguin Books Ltd, Registered Offices: 80 Strand, London WC2R 0RL, England
For more information about the Penguin Group visit penguin.com

First published in Spainish under the title *Jenni Rivera: La increíble vida de una mariposa guerrera* by C.A. Press, a member of Penguin Group (USA) Inc., 2013
This English-language edition published 2013

Translation by Diane Stockwell

ISBN 978-0-14-751053-2

Printed in the United States of America
10 9 8 7 6 5 4 3 2 1

To the memory of Jenni Rivera and all the

"Warrior Butterflies" who persevere

no matter what the odds.

Contents

CONTENTS

Bury Me with the Band

El día en que yo me muera
que me entierren con la banda

—From the song
"Que me entierren con la banda"
(Bury Me with the Band)
by Antonio Aguilar,
performed by Jenni Rivera and Lupillo Rivera

On the morning of her death, Dolores Janney Rivera Saavedra woke up feeling great. The night before, she had performed to a sellout crowd in Colima, Mexico, and she would be at the Monterrey Arena that night.

For Rivera, this was a very important show. With 16,000 seats, the Monterrey Arena is one of the biggest, most prestigious venues in Mexico. Jenni had done a concert there once before, and it had sold out. For this one, she had decided to place the stage in the very center of the arena floor—creating a 360-degree stage, like a bullfight ring—to fit more seats, and to have a more intimate atmosphere. Tickets had sold out in less than fifteen days, quite an accomplishment, and Jenni felt that she had a tremendous responsibility to the audience in Monterrey, especially now that she was a judge on *La Voz . . . Mexico*, and was seen on television by millions of viewers every week.

She had enthusiastically, painstakingly planned the concerts down to the last detail. Her band and the mariachi group that accompanied her on her *ranchero* songs would also travel from

Colima. She had her carefully chosen wardrobe with her, ranging from a sumptuous pink gown with a diagonal floral pattern, to a super-tight pair of jeans and jacket that hugged every inch of her generous curves. Each wardrobe change corresponded perfectly to the music, which also reflected the many facets of Rivera: party girl, classy lady, grand diva, best friend.

That Saturday afternoon, as she arrived in Monterrey, Rivera was all of those things. Her trusted inner circle was with her, including Arturo Rivera, her long-time publicist and one of the most popular public relations agents in Mexico. Jenni trusted his judgment implicitly, and considered him her right-hand man who helped her go to battle with the media when necessary. And there was her makeup artist, Yacob Yenale, a Mexican living in Los Angeles who worked with all of the "greats," from Christina Aguilera to Rihanna, but he was such close pals with Rivera he cleared his whole calendar just so he could travel all over Mexico at her side. Jorge Gonzalez was her stylist, in charge of maintaining the very long, exquisite extensions that had become Jenni's trademark. From her management team, on this trip Rivera traveled with her lawyer, Mario Macias.

The mood was festive when they landed. Things could not have been going any better for Rivera. Colima had been a smashing success, and Monterrey should be even bigger. And the next day, on Sunday, they would be on the set of *La Voz*, for the semifinals of the talent show in search of Mexico's next great voice. Rivera was feeling so good, she had even made plans to go out after her concert. The band M-40 also had a show in Monterrey that night, and she had asked their promoter to reserve a VIP table for her at the club where they were performing. Jenni liked to support up-and-coming acts—over the years she had strongly supported artists like Akwid, Larry Hernandez, Espinoza Paz, 3BallMTY—and M-40 was starting to make a name for themselves.

The promoter set aside not just one but four tables for Jenni and her entourage, and he even had a disguise waiting for her, so that no one would recognize her. He had also reserved four hotel rooms for her, which as things turned out would go unused. After they landed in Monterrey, Jenni and her group headed straight to the arena for a sound check, which got delayed because the band and the mariachis hadn't arrived from Colima yet. Jenni always traveled with her own band: La Banda Divina de Jenni Rivera. The group lived in Mazatlan, and they toured with her throughout Mexico and the United States, along with sound, lighting, video, and pyrotechnics technicians, and her production director, Rudy Echauri. Although when she was just getting her start, Jenni had hired local mariachi musicians to keep costs down, over the last year her star had risen so high that she could afford to bring the same mariachi group along on tour to perform on most of the major concert stages in Mexico.

The sound check wouldn't be finished until almost eight o'clock that evening. Jenni was so happy with the sound quality and the venue that she told her promoter she wanted to come back and do another show in February. They even picked out a tentative date: February 16th.

That night, Rivera arrived at the arena ready to give the show of her life. It was always like that, but on that particular night you could really feel the electricity in the air.

She stepped out onto the stage dressed all in black, wearing a formfitting dress and a short leather jacket. She wore high heels and a long necklace. Her hair, styled by Gonzalez, fell in a golden, cascading mane down her back, almost reaching her waist.

"Ladies, when we drink tequila we get loose!" she exclaimed, raising a glass to the crowd. "Here's to getting loose!" she yelled to the sellout throng.

At the end of the night, after she had worn her stunning gowns, after the tears had streamed down her cheeks as she sang her most sentimental *rancheras*, she got a big surprise: executives from her record label, Fonovisa, took the stage to present her with Gold and Platinum records, commemorating the stellar sales of her two latest albums. It was the icing on the cake for a special night, which could not have gone any better.

"Ay, *m'ija*, I'm happy, so happy," she said at the press conference after the show. "I'm so happy . . . all the times I've been knocked down, I've gotten back up. God is good and He never lets go of my hand. And I have my fans, who support me, and live with me, and want to see me do well."

Once the press conference was over, Jenni and her team were supposed to go to the hotel or to the M-40 show. But at some point there was a change of plans. Now they wouldn't spend the night at the hotel or partying at the club. Jenni would go back to Mexico City that very night; she had to be at the Televisa studios at eleven o'clock sharp the next morning to start taping *La Voz*, and she must not have wanted to run the risk of arriving late. So she decided to make the trip right after her show, so she would be in Mexico City bright and early the next morning and keep right on working. The travel arrangements were made so last-minute that when her lawyer Macias called her production director Rudy Echauri to let him know he could go along with them in a private jet, Echauri didn't get the message in time. He was at his hotel, taking a shower. By the time he checked his messages it was too late, the group had already left. He stuck to his original plan, returning to Mexico City on a commercial Volaris airlines flight.

Once the show and the press conference were over, Rivera and the group traveling with her got in the car that would take them to the airport, without Echauri, and without Alejandra Guzman, who Jenni had also invited to fly with them on the private jet. But Alejandra decided to take a commercial flight as she had originally planned, because she was traveling with her boyfriend.

From the backseat of the car driving to the airport, Yenale, the makeup artist, took a picture of the group on his cell phone and posted it on the Internet. Everyone smiled brightly, the joy on their faces shining through.

"On our way back to Mexico City . . . Jenni Rivera, Arturo, Gigi and me. I love youoouu!!" he posted along with the photo.

On the drive to the airport, Jenni used the time to answer messages and tweets. One was from Javier Estrella, a friend and Televisa reporter who had gotten concerned after seeing her cry during the concert.

"Jenni, please tell me you're okay?" he wrote at 12:27.

"Really I'm at peace!" she answered him at 3:09 in the morning. "I'm so happy . . . I'm fine . . . I promise. Some songs just make me cry. That's all."

"God is with me. I trust in Him," she added a minute later.

"My respect and admiration for you," Estrella replied at 3:11. "Have a good night a great trip to Mexico City!"

Exactly four minutes later, the Learjet numbered N3445MC set off for Mexico City, and Rivera had to turn off her cell phone. The jet had been made in 1969—it was forty-three years old—but Jenni would not have known that. And she would not have known that her pilot, Manuel Perez Soto, was seventy-eight years old, or that his copilot, Alejandro Torres, was only twenty.

The jet took off into the dark sky over Monterrey, now gone quiet after Jenni's show. It was a clear night, with no rain, and five minutes into the flight, at 28,000 feet, the city lights began to fade into the distance.

Maybe Rivera had closed her eyes, tired after such a long day. Maybe she stayed up to talk with her friends, since it was a short flight; they would be in Toluca, just outside of Mexico City, in only an hour. In any case, at around 3:19 in the morning something went wrong, and the Learjet, which had so gracefully taken to the air, suddenly stalled. Its flight was abruptly interrupted, like a bird colliding with a glass door. The jet shuddered, indecisive, and without warning went down, reaching a speed of 1,000 kilometers an hour.

It happened so fast, Jenni and the others probably did not even have time to notice that anything was terribly wrong. The Learjet mercilessly crashed to the Mexican ground, and at 3:20 AM, the air traffic control tower reported that they had lost contact with the aircraft.

Jenni Rivera, forty-three years old, lay dead in a remote ranch on the outskirts of Monterrey, far from the arena that had wrapped her in thunderous applause just hours before.

JENNI
RIVERA

CHAPTER 1

The Rivera Dynasty

The Rivera Dynasty. The Riveras. La Familia Rivera. That's what people called them. "La Familia," "The Clan," in capital letters, as if they were a sacred tribe, or royalty, or nobility. When they were seen together, the myth only grew: Don Pedro Rivera, the patriarch who's hand and vision had molded his children's destinies; Lupillo, in his expensive suits, instantly recognizable with his shaved head and mustache; Pedro Jr., the charismatic preacher; Rosie, the little sister, a beauty, with a face like a lovely, fair, blonde Madonna; Juan and Gustavo, also singers; and Jenni, curvaceous and exuberant, with full lips and a big smile. They talked about the mother—Doña Rosa—who was rarely seen, like in traditional Italian families where the mothers were powerful, but silent figures. It was assumed she must have been a woman of steel to have raised a brood of children with such strong personalities, although she rarely made any public statements.

Each one led their own lives independently, but once in a while "The Riveras" would appear together, and they were something to behold. The men in their Mexican sombreros, boots and macho attitude; and her, Jenni, a dose of pure femininity: a curvy figure, with flawless makeup, long, always carefully styled hair, tight, but tasteful dresses, bright-colored outfits — purples, reds and blues — or dressed all in black, a color she wore so well. It was impressive just to watch them interact, since each one had their own distinct personality and their own space, and they were mutually respectful of one another. When The Riveras were together, no one dominated the conversation, no one interrupted the others, or openly disagreed. One seamlessly picked up where the other left off, like runners in a relay race. If one stood out from the rest, it was Don Pedro, for his sentimentality. It was not unusual to see him shed a few heartfelt tears during interviews.

The Rivera Family was unified, and loyal. They must have had their disagreements in private, misunderstandings must have flared up when so many strong personalities were together in one room. But seen from the outside, they were an unbreakable chain, with every link supporting the next. If the press criticized one — and that happened very often — the others pounced like a pack of wolves to defend their own. Each could retreat to their own corner, and take care of their own business, but woe be it to anyone who messed with their brother, their sister, their father, their blood.

Jenni said it herself in the press conference the night of her death, when she was asked if she ever fought with Lupillo, her most famous brother.

"As siblings we don't always agree on everything, and we both have our tempers, more than any of the others," she answered

4

with her characteristic candor. "But whenever I've had a really big problem in my life my brother forgets everything, whatever disagreement or hurt feeling and he talks to me and says, 'sister, I'm with you.'"

The Riveras. On the day of Jenni's funeral, at the Gibson Amphitheatre in Los Angeles, the family dressed all in red and white, they looked like kings, princes and princesses, so dignified, so tasteful and, above all, so eloquent. From the eldest, Don Pedro, right down to the youngest, Jenni's son Johnny, they spoke with the natural ease and the expressive vocabulary of those who are either highly educated, or have grown up in an environment surrounded by excellent orators. But the Riveras weren't royalty or nobility. Unlike other musical families, like the Aguilars or the Fernandez family—their artistic story had barely begun, since the biggest stars weren't the father, but the children—Lupillo and Jenni. As far as money, education or any kind of aristocratic lineage went, the family had started out with absolutely none of those things.

As Jenni said herself over and over again over the years, "No one opened any doors for me. I pushed them all open for myself."

And what doors she had opened. On the day she died, Jenni Rivera was the highest-selling artist at her record label, the multinational Fonovisa, and she was the highest selling female artist in regional Mexican music, period. Among female performers of all genres, she toured the most, and she was the only Latina artist who had her own weekly radio program (*Contacto directo* con Jenni Rivera, on Entravision), her own reality television show (*I Love Jenni*, on Mun2), her own makeup and clothing lines, and her own foundation (the Jenni Rivera Love Foundation). To top it off, just weeks before her death, Rivera had signed a contract with ABC to produce and star in her own weekly television series *in English*. It was an unprecedented achievement for a Latin music artist. Jenni Rivera was on the brink of superstardom, and she knew it.

"Two thousand thirteen was going to be an incredible year," Pete Salgado, who had been Rivera's manager since 2004, told *Billboard*. "Our contract with ABC was going to be the first of its kind; she was going to be the first Latina to have her own series. And we were going to do it her way, with her as the producer. There were going to be a lot of 'firsts.' [. . .] At our production company, we were all really focused, aggressive, we were in the game. She was ready. And 2013 was going to be her year to be a mom. She was always saying she had spent so many years being the one supporting her children—like a dad—that now was the time to be a mom. Mom in the best sense of the word: cooking breakfast for her kids, taking them to school, going to conferences with their teachers. That's why I say there's no time to be sad. We have to finish what we started. We have to make sure her legacy goes on. Those kinds of artists come along once a generation. Jenni is unique. It's going to be a long time before someone comes along who even comes close."

The intention to keep Jenni's legacy alive was clear at her funeral service, where many of her family members talked about her in the present tense, as if she were physically still there with them. No one was more moving than her son Johnny Lopez, eleven years old, and the last to speak, after all the rest of the family. "This is the hardest thing that I have ever had to go through in my entire life," he said, letting out a sigh, already demonstrating the Rivera clan's characteristic poise. "I've had a short eleven years with my mom," Johnny said. "But through those short eleven years she tried her best to set the best example that she could." said Johnny, an adorable boy with round cheeks. "I have never seen a mother work so hard to accomplish everything, even get the groceries for her kids." he went on, occasionally wiping at the tears streaming down his cheeks. "It's a real honor to say that Jenni Rivera, the person that everyone is talking about, is my mom. That she lives on in me."

CHAPTER
2

Let Me Live

J enni Rivera never wanted to be a singer. She never dreamed about it, never imagined it, never pursued it, and for a long time she didn't even want to sing. The one who had really wanted to be a singer was her father, Pedro Rivera, a humble man who had taken his first steps as a singer and composer back in La Barca, Jalisco, Mexico, in the early sixties. Pedro Rivera was a young man with a compact build, black hair and a mustache, and an easy, bright smile. He was short, and he compensated for this by always wearing a white cowboy hat, adding height. He never wore the traditional Mexican cowboy outfit and accessories that many banda and norteño singers did. Rivera was classy. He was always impeccably dressed, from his earliest beginnings up to the present, with his formfitting pants and shirt, leather belt, and boots polished to a high luster. Years later his careful self-presentation would be emulated by his children, Jenni and Lupillo, and his excellent people skills and talent for public speaking would also be passed down to them. Pedro Rivera was always doing public relations, trying to get to know people in the business—promoters, artists and record label executives—who could open doors.

Pedro didn't come from a musical family, and no one close to him sang when he was growing up. His father was in the military, and was sometimes away from home for months at a time. And they were poor. In an interview with *La Opinion* in 2002, Pedro recalled that his grandfather in Jalisco would say, "We're of the goats at the back of the herd." He meant that "when we tended those animals, the skinniest, hungriest goats were the ones that were always lagging behind the rest of the herd."

Poor or not, Pedro was drawn to music. Wanting to find his place in that world, he set out for the city of Hermosillo in Sinaloa on his bicycle. There he met Rosa Amelia Saavedra, a dark beauty from Sinaloa who entered singing contests for fans of the local radio station XEDL AM.

They married in 1963. Pedro took his young wife to Guadalajara, where they lived at a truck stop for three months. He tried to make a living washing cars and trucks, but his earnings were barely enough to keep them alive, and the young couple was hungry.

Later, Pedro remembered in the interview with *La Opinion*, "we went back to Hermosillo, and they locked me up in jail, accusing me of robbery. I was in the local prison for two months, and I got out thanks to my own wife's efforts. Then I started selling lottery tickets and tacos made with turtle meat."

Finally, Pedro decided to try his luck up North in the United States. That would have been in 1964, according to a *La Opinion* article published in 2002—although Pedro's Facebook page gives the date as April 19, 1966, the same day as the death of his idol, Javier Solis. No matter the year, Rivera crossed the border as an undocumented immigrant and took a freight train from Yuma, Arizona to Indio, California. Once in Indio, a man gave him a ride in his car to Los Angeles. But initially that was not his final destination. Pedro then took a bus with some other immigrants headed for Fresno, where he was hired to work at Rancho Coit, a farm, picking lettuce, melons, grapes and strawberries. Rosa stayed behind in Mexico, and eventually she made her way North to join her husband.

Years later, once he was famous, Pedro would call himself *El Patriarca del Corrido*, *El Cantante del Pueblo* and *El Personaje del Pueblo*, all names stemming directly from life experiences he would never forget, and which always stayed with him.

"I've always tried to be the best at whatever I'm doing," Pedro states in his Facebook bio. "I'm a man with a fighting spirit, hardworking, with strong convictions, a strong character, very determined. I still remember herding the goats in my native Jalisco, believing that someday I would do great things and would achieve a better future, in spite of my limited education."

Pedro and Rosa already had a son, Juan, when Rosa got pregnant again in 1968. She carried in her womb her first daughter: Jenni.

The pregnancy with Jenni had come as a surprise. The Riveras were still struggling financially, and having another baby on the way made their plans to start a new life in a different country especially challenging. The situation was even more complicated bearing in mind that Pedro and his family had no way to cross the border legally. They were poor Mexican workers, like so many others in search of their own American dream.

They did not have the money or the knowledge required to apply for tourist or worker visas. Pedro had already made the first crossing a few years earlier, and now he and his family had decided to cross over permanently. Life would be better up North. The decision to take a huge chance, to cross the border illegally once again, with a baby on the way, and settle in the United States instead of staying in Mexico—the land of his family, his grandmother, and his language—surely played a critical role in Jenni's development as a person, and later, as an artist.

"I was born here [in the United States]," Jenni told me on *Estudio Billboard*, a television show featuring interviews and performances with Latino artists broadcast on the V-Me network in the United States and on Fox Life and other channels throughout Latin America. "My mother was pregnant with me when she crossed the border, and the last thing she wanted then was to have a baby. They were going to the United States to triumph, to find a better future for the family." Having a baby under those circumstances was very hard, but Jenni would not be denied: "I fought to stay in my mother's womb, because I wanted other things. That's when the fight of my life began. And I got here, and I stayed."

The song "Déjame vivir," (Let me Live), that Rivera wrote for her album *Parrandera, Rebelde y Atrevida*, was inspired by her life's beginnings, and tells the story of a baby inside his mother's womb who asks her to let him live, saying: *"Think of what I could be / a little box of surprises if you let me live / Maybe someday I'll be someone important, someone who makes you laugh."*

Rivera never talked in any detail about what her mother's situation actually was, or how similar it may have been to the story in the song she would sing years later. What's certain is that, like so many other things she talked about through her songs, those lyrics would uncannily reflect real life. Jenni really did turn out to be a box full of surprises. Yes, she would grow up to be someone important, far beyond their wildest dreams. No father or mother could imagine that a daughter could reach such great heights. The fact that she was the daughter of poor, marginalized illegal Mexican immigrants made it all the more surreal.

J enni Rivera was not born in Long Beach, as has often been reported. She was born in Culver City, an area on the west side of Los Angeles surrounded by wealthy communities like Santa Monica, Pacific Palisades and Venice Beach. Sony Pictures Studio, which was MGM Studios when Jenni lived there, was located in Culver City, along with The Culver Studios and Balboa Records. Five miles to the east was Beverly Hills, the legendary neighborhood home to millionaires and movie stars, and six miles to the west were Santa Monica and Venice Beach, where every house with a view of the ocean costs a sizeable fortune. Even in Culver City itself, some homes sell for millions of dollars, just a few blocks away from cramped apartment buildings where several families can share a single room. In other words, the Riveras lived just minutes away from luxury, splendor and Hollywood dreams, but they were so far away from that world, they may as well have been living on Mars.

Jenni was born on July 2, 1969. The name her parents put on her birth certificate was Dolores Janney Rivera Saavedra, effectively stamping their daughter with a bicultural, bilingual identity from the moment of her birth. "Janney," which later became "Jenni," was clearly a nod to their new country where English was spoken. And Dolores, of course, is a quintessentially Mexican name, of Spanish origin, which means "one who suffers pain in remembering the pain the Virgin Mary suffered because of the death of her son." And that definition, ironically and sadly, would characterize its bearer.

The Riveras lived in a small walk-up apartment building, just a few stories high, that are so common throughout Southern California. The apartment was small, and they had plenty of noisy neighbors. Rosa played music so Jenni wouldn't be awakened by all the noise from the outside. So ever since her infancy, music was a constant in her life, starting with Mexican music more than anything.

Being Mexican in the United States was hardly unusual, and Jenni picked up on this quickly. She grew up in a very Mexican environment, even though they were in the heart of Los Angeles. But her parents were strict; for example, they did not allow their children to speak English at home. "At home I spoke Spanish, ate Mexican food, and listened to Mexican music, like Lola Beltran, Pedro Infante, Vicente Fernandez, Lupita D'Alessio, all those artists who are real legends," Jenni told me on *Estudio Billboard* in 2010. "And they instilled in me what Mexican music was, what my roots were. My dad would throw a fit if he came home and the radio was tuned to hip-hop, music in English and he had left it on the Spanish, Mexican station. I was allowed to speak English at school. And at home, they were going to raise me like a Mexican girl."

But in spite of being raised like a Mexican girl, growing up in the Rivera family must have been a tremendously liberating experience for a girl of Jenni Rivera's character. Doña Rosa was a traditional, conservative Mexican mother, but she expected all of her children, including her daughters, to study hard and excel at school. Jenni's exceptional intelligence was obvious, and Doña Rosa expected only the best from her. Her goal for her daughter was that she would one day go to college, which she herself had not been able to do, and become someone important: a teacher, a psychologist, a nurse.

For his part, Don Pedro was strict, upstanding, demanding, and a typically macho Mexican in every way. But he would do anything for his little Jenni. And she would do anything for him. Over the course of her career, Jenni's close bond with her father was undeniable. When she spoke of him her voice softened, her defenses dropped, she couldn't help but smile. Jenni Rivera loved her father, and her father loved her. Maybe he loved her so very much because she was his first daughter among his sons, and she would be the only girl for quite a while, until Rosie arrived years later. He always treated her like a little princess, but he also taught her to be just as strong and self-reliant as any man.

When Jenni was still very small, the Riveras moved from Culver City to Long Beach, a big step up in the world, since they went from living in an apartment to a house. But the neighborhood may have been less desirable than the one they left behind. The new house was in the western part of Long Beach, near Hill Street and Gale Avenue, in an area known for its gangs. But Long Beach in general was also known for its diversity. Today, of the hundred largest cities in the United States, it is considered the most diverse, ethnically and culturally.

"To us, it was a good neighborhood," Jenni commented, while talking about the area where she grew up in an interview with Omar Argueta for *La Cronica* in 2002. "But it was a ghetto. I like that we grew up in such a diverse neighborhood. Our friends were Samoan, Filipino, black, of all races. But there were fights and shootings. And when everyone got older and we went to Stevens Junior High, each race broke off into their own gang. Someone was always picking on us just because we were another race."

Jenni spoke very openly about her childhood many times. The family had little money, and everyone worked. In an interview published by *La Opinion* on August 8, 2001, Jenni said that her mother worked in a factory, and the other children collected cans in the streets to redeem them. Jenni went to school and took care of her younger siblings, because there was no money to hire a babysitter. Even though they were poor, and the neighborhood wasn't the safest, Rivera always recalled her childhood as an especially happy time in her life.

"Financially, I wasn't born a queen of queens," Rivera once said. "But in my house my father always taught me that I was a queen. Yes, I was the queen of the house, and later I would be the queen of Long Beach, according to my dad, and later the queen of California, of the United States, of Mexico. My dad always showed me lots of affection as a child. I was the first girl of four children, before Rosie. And my father was always showing his affection, and I grew up with lots of love."

Just as Pedro Rivera always insisted on treating his daughter like a princess, he made sure that she had the same attitude and strong backbone as her brothers. His little Jenni was a princess, but she was a princess who could take care of herself out there in the world, as well as or even better than any man.

"I was very close to Jenni because she was a very feisty child, very happy, and I liked being around her," Pedro Rivera said in an interview on the Univision television show *Primer Impacto*. "She would say she wasn't the prettiest, but she was the toughest. One time she came home from school crying and I say 'What's wrong, what happened?' and she says 'A girl who's bigger than me hit me.' And I tell her, 'Go back and teach her that *no one* is going to hit you.' So she went back to school and right in front of the teacher, she grabbed the bigger girl, and she had her mind made up, she grabbed her and knocked her down on the floor, put her foot right on her throat, and pulled her hair hard. She was ready to kill her right there," Don Pedro added, chuckling.

Jenni was taught to never let anyone push her around. If she were to live among men, she had to know how to defend herself among men. Many years later, when her star was starting to rise, Jenni began to get a reputation as a woman who would not let anyone step on her, not the media, or the record industry or anyone else; she became known as a woman who said exactly what she thought and felt and would never let anyone twist her arm. Those traits were surely forged back in those early years in Long Beach.

"I don't know any other life apart from that," Jenni said. "My parents and my brothers raised me to be very strong, not docile, not very feminine or sweet," she recalled. "I played marbles, I played baseball. I did whatever my four brothers did. They went around getting into trouble and I would go along with them, and sometimes do it even better. It wasn't hard because that's how I was raised. I didn't have any other choice."

When she was asked in an interview if she had been the kind of little girl that played with dolls, Jenni laughed. "My mom wished with all of her heart, with all of her soul that I would be one of those girls," she said. "So she saved up some money to buy the little girl of the house her little dolls, and little kitchen toys. My brothers burned my little dolls, they broke them. They broke my little cups and plates too. They wanted me to ride bikes with them, they wanted me to be good at playing marbles. I was a champion at marbles. So when my mom would ask, 'M'ija, what do you want me to buy for you?' I wanted a lawn mower."

Jenni may not have been a typical little girl playing with dolls and throwing little hissy fits, but she was a very good student, and she always earned good grades. From elementary school up to the years she attended Long Beach Poly high school, Jenni stood out as an excellent student, getting straight As. The fact that she did so well even though English was not her first language made her academic achievements even more extraordinary. Jenni was a whiz kid. Learning came easily to her. Since she was so dedicated to her schoolwork, there was little time left over for boyfriends or other interests. And back then, Jenni was a chubby, plain girl, with dark hair and little makeup, very different from the sophisticated, sensual and always fabulously put together Jenni that the world would come to know.

"I didn't have lots of boyfriends," she said in the same interview. "I was the ugly duckling of my friends and the whole school. I focused on my studies, I really, really liked to study. My grades were always tens. Tens for academics, and for behavior. I behaved very well in school, and nobody tried to pick fights with me anymore, and I could really fight because my brothers had taught me," Jenni said with a laugh. "So there wasn't much time and there really weren't any boys who were interested in me."

Maybe there weren't any "boys" who were interested in Jenni, but there was one young man who was very interested in her. His name was Jose Trinidad Marin, who everyone called "Trino." He was twenty-one years old, six years older than Jenni, who was barely fifteen at the time, and in the tenth grade at Long Beach Poly. For a young girl who had never had a boyfriend, the attentions of a good-looking, older Mexican man were hard to resist. Jenni, the conscientious student who always earned tens in everything, fell in love. Or, as she would put it years later, she thought she was in love. In any case, at fifteen, the princess of the Rivera family got pregnant, and left home to live with her boyfriend. On June 26, 1985, after Jenni had turned sixteen, she gave birth to her first child, a little girl, Janney Marin Rivera, nicknamed "Chiquis."

Just then, Jenni could have dropped out of school for good and just been a mom, the destiny of so many teens from poor families who get pregnant. She had already left home to live with her boyfriend and their baby. But Jenni knew very well she wanted to do something more with her life. She stayed together with Trino, and tried to be a good partner, a good mother, and still a good student.

"Usually, when a teenage girl gets pregnant, she drops out of school," Rivera told Argueta in *La Cronica*. "I thought that's what would happen to me too, but the counselors at my school told me they would not let me drop out under any circumstance. They said I had too much promise."

But Long Beach Poly wasn't the best school for a girl in Jenni's situation. It was an excellent high school, with acclaimed programs in art, athletics, and, ironically, music. But as the most important, and oldest high school in the city, it was also the largest, with over 5,000 students.

Jenni finished out tenth grade there, and then enrolled in Reid Continuation High School. Reid is a school for students who have had to interrupt their studies for one reason or another. It was a much smaller, more personal place than Poly. On its Web page, the school describes itself as "a credit-recovery, alternative program for students who want a different educational experience culminating in a diploma. The staff at Reid collaborate to provide a safe, nurturing environment in which students are encouraged to become socially accountable global citizens. Students will develop respect for themselves and others as well as create a transition plan for the next phase of their life. [. . .] Our staff is committed to making graduation a reality for our students who may have been tempted to drop out of school after falling behind in credits. We ask our students to believe in themselves as we believe in them."

Rivera had never needed any special attention, or an environment that would nurture her growth. But now, with a baby, everything had changed.

"I stayed in school, even though I got pregnant at fifteen, and had my daughter when I was sixteen," Jenni said in a television interview with the journalist Susana Heredia for *TVNotas*. "And there was no time for dances or sports. I went straight home after school, to cook, to be a mom, a wife, and when I graduated, my daughter was two years old."

Not only did Rivera graduate on time, she was first in her class. At that point, once again she could have decided to take a break from her education and be a stay-at-home mom. And once again, she opted to continue on her path in search of a better life. She first enrolled in Long Beach City College, a junior college where any high school graduate could enroll. But she soon transferred to Long Beach State University, where she graduated in 1991 with a degree in Business Administration.

Around then Rivera went through a very dark time. When she was pregnant for the second time with her daughter Jacqueline Melina Campos, she had fought with Trino and had left their home.

"For a while I lived in an unheated garage with my oldest daughter, who was four years old at the time; I was seven months' pregnant," she told *La Opinion* in a 2001 interview. "I was too proud to go back to my parents' house during this rough time, when my husband had thrown me out."

Her troubles didn't stop there. Jenni had had problems with Trino almost from the start.

"The violence started as soon as I moved in with him," Jenni said in a television interview on *Escándalo TV*. "He claimed the baby wasn't his. He made it impossible for me to stay at home, beaten down when all of my teachers told me I had talent, and I knew I was going to go far. I suffered a great deal of physical abuse from him."

At eighteen, in a state of utter despair and not seeing any way out of her desperate circumstances, Jenni tried to kill herself. "I wanted to study, to get ahead, but I couldn't do it, it seemed impossible," Jenni said on *Escándalo TV*. "I had my daughter and I was working, and I took a lot of pills to end it all. When I opened my eyes again, my mother and father were next to my bed in the hospital, asking, 'Why?'"

In spite of everything, Jenni stayed with Trino, and went back to living with him after going through that time living in a cold garage on her own with Chiquis. She had Jacquie on November 30, 1989, four years after her older sister; her third child, Trinidad "Michael" Angelo Rivera was born on September 11, 1991. Years later, Trinidad would change his name to Michael, after his father was sentenced to prison for abusing his own daughter and Jenni's younger sister.

At twenty-one years old, Jenni already had a college degree, but she also already had three children ranging in age from her newborn son to her six-year-old daughter.

Almost twenty years later, on *TVNotas* Susana Heredia asked her what her parents had thought about what she was going through, and if she had been very in love with Trino during that time.

"Well, what could they think, because I really gave it to them good," she said with a smile. "And they really suffered. Especially my father, whose little princess had grown up so fast." As for Trino: "At fifteen I don't know if you can call it love," she said. "You're dazzled. No one noticed me at all. He was the first who noticed. And he was six years older than me. I can't tell you it was love, because when I was pregnant, during the first three months I had a lot of nausea, a lot of things made me sick, and he was one of those things that turned my stomach. I couldn't even see him, I couldn't stand it, but since I had already gotten my Sunday 7," she said, using an old Latina expression referring to Sunday, the

7th day as bad luck, a euphemism for getting pregnant without wanting to, or suffering some misfortune. "And your parents teach you that the first man you're with, is the one you'll stay with."

Like so many other women—Latinas or not—as a teenager Jenni thought it was her duty to stick by her husband, no matter what. That's how she had been raised.

"I knew when I was in that relationship that something wasn't right, but I thought I had to stay with him, just like my mother and my grandmother," she told *Escándalo TV*. "I didn't want to be alone, I believed that marriage was forever."

And Rivera stayed with Trino, until she couldn't anymore. In 1992 she left him, alleging that he had been abusive. But it was more than that. Jenni was no longer the little fifteen-year-old who had gotten pregnant. She was a professional, self-sufficient, self-assured woman. She had succeeded and moved ahead in ways her partner never imagined, while he had stayed in the same place.

"Our relationship was a difficult one, where not only I suffered, but he suffered too," Jenni told me on *Estudio Billboard* in 2010. "Because I can't say that I was only a victim. I was an aggressor too because I didn't know what else to do. I didn't know how to get out so he would never hit me again. But when we separated and I started to sing, he started always telling me that I couldn't do it, that I'd never amount to anything."

When Trino saw that Jenni was starting to have some success and could spread her wings and fly on her own, he couldn't stand it. "Even once we were separated, I went through some hard times with him because he couldn't stand that I was now a butterfly in flight, not the little caterpillar that he was so used to stepping on," Jenni told me on *Estudio Billboard*, referring to her hit "Mariposa Guerrera," (Warrior Butterfly), that was inspired by this period in her life. "And it was really hard but you know, over the years I've realized that God lets you go through certain experiences in your life because maybe at some point you will be able to help someone else who's going through it, or another woman who's going through it."

What Jenni did not know at the time was that Trino had not only been physically abusing her, he had also sexually abused their eldest daughter, Chiquis, and Jenni's own younger sister, Rosie, who she adored as if she were her daughter.

But that discovery would come later, after Trino had already gotten out of their lives. It's no coincidence that Jenni finally started to sing during this phase in her life. At the time, she was a single mother who, aside from not having a man by her side, had been abused and deceived in the most despicable ways. Jenni would report Trino to the authorities, but years would pass before he was captured, put on trial, and sentenced to prison.

For now, Jenni was alone. But she had been a warrior in her childhood and adolescence, and she would be an even stronger one now. Jenni Rivera was only twenty-two years old, and she had already lived a whole life, but her career was just starting to take flight.

CHAPTER 3

The Roots of Success

D on Pedro had always wanted his daughter to sing. It was partly a typical father's pride, and partly, Pedro, who had a great eye for talent, sensed there was something very special about his daughter. But ever since she was small, Jenni had been a businesswoman. As a little girl in elementary school, she had sold gum to make money. In her interview with Omar Argueta published in *La Cronica*, she said the first and only time she had sung in public was when she was eleven, in a talent contest in Long Beach. "My dad got mad at me, not because I didn't win, but because I got so scared I couldn't finish," Rivera said. "He always taught us not to give up."

Jenni wouldn't sing again for another eleven years. In the meantime, she got together with Trino, had Chiquis, Jackie and Michael, graduated from high school, and graduated from college. She got her real estate license and, gradually, as a single mother, Jenni started to earn a comfortable living. She was a good saleswoman, and selling houses brought in a decent income. She could support her children just fine, with or without a man.

For his part, Pedro Rivera had also started to get ahead in music. Although he had held all kinds of jobs since first arriving in the United States, music was still his main objective and his passion, and he tried to work in it any way he could.

In the early seventies, he started to work even harder at pursuing music, and in 1971, while listening to the radio, the host Humberto Luna announced a contest for aspiring singers in El Monte, sponsored by Bill McGuire Chevrolet. Pedro immediately saw an opportunity, and wrote down the details. It was a memorable experience for him because the judge of the contest was Angelo Gonzalez, a songwriter who had written "La silla vacía" and "Sin fortuna."

Pedro didn't win, but that was just the beginning.

The following year, in 1974, he joined forces with another singer, Apolinar Hernández, and they began performing as a duo, calling themselves Los Arrieros. But of all of his various jobs, the most productive for Pedro in terms of his fledgling musical career was working as a photographer.

"I sang and wrote songs, but no one was listening," Pedro recalled. Almost by accident, he started taking pictures at a place called La Hacienda in Long Beach. "First, I got to be friends with the bar's owners, and then I would show up on Wednesdays when people at the bar would get up and sing, and when there was no one to sing, the emcee would say, 'There's no one to sing, let's get the photographer up here to sing.' It got to the point where customers started asking the photographer to sing."

His big break came in 1984, the year the Olympics were held in Los Angeles. Rivera, always the entrepreneur, had the brilliant idea of selling buttons commemorating the Olympics for

$1. With the support of his wife and children, who now numbered six, he sold 14,000 buttons. He invested the earnings on the production of his first record, *Voy a bajarte una estrella*, which he sang accompanied by a mariachi band.

"It's the hard times that give you energy, the strength to keep going, that's when you get ideas, and unexpected things start to happen," he said in an interview on the TV Azteca show *El Pelado de la Noche*, talking about what he was able to do when he really didn't have any resources, evoking the same sentiment his daughter would talk about so many times in her life. "You have to really want it, you have to do things with enthusiasm."

From 1984 on, Pedro's luck in music started to change, and for the first time his name was getting out there. Pedro, who had worked so hard to be somebody in music, started to get cast as an actor in small roles in Mexican movies. More importantly, some of the corridos, songs that tell stories, that he had composed were used in the soundtracks of these movies.

Pedro had first begun working in the movies when he was hired to be a still photographer for the film *Asalto* en Tijuana. In 1985, he landed a small acting part in the film *La tumba del mojado*, with Humberto Luna, Miguel Angel Rodriguez and Pedro Infante Jr. And in 1986 he got another small role in *Verdugo de traidores*, starring Mario Almada and Sergio Goyri. Pedro also wrote the song "Verdugo de traidores," and in 1987 his song "Camino al infierno" inspired the movie of the same name, which featured Los Tigres del Norte and Sergio Goyri.

The pinnacle moment of this period in Pedro Rivera's life came in 1987, when he launched his own record label, Cintas Acuario. The inspiration for this came to him through his work as a nightclub photographer, when one evening he met a young singer named Genaro Rodriguez.

"Cintas Acuario got started because a young man named Genaro Rodriguez gave me a master produced by Paulino Vargas," Pedro explained in a 2011 interview with his friend, the actor Octavio Acosta. "The master was released by Eco Musical, but it wasn't successful, and the master was returned to the artist. And at a photography studio, they told me that I could make thousands and thousands of cassettes from that master."

From that very first master, Pedro produced a cassette of corridos, and from then on, when he was taking one of his photos in the nightclubs, he would offer the customers the cassette to purchase along with the picture. The business started to catch on, and gradually other artists and bands would give him their masters so that Pedro could sell their cassettes in the clubs too.

"First was el Chapo de Sinaloa in 1986. Then Los Razos in '87, little by little it started to work," Pedro told Octavio Acosta. "We didn't have anyone to listen to us, to take care of us, or help us. We were all drifting around in the street, and whoever stuck around, stuck around. Like I did. The career I've made is more about longevity than talent. It's staying and staying and staying, you're always there until something clicks."

It was never easy, especially at the beginning.

Pedro would manufacture cassettes for the then-unknown artists with the masters they gave him. He sent the cassettes to a distributor, taking whatever was left over to local flea markets on the weekends, where he sold them at a little stand.

Jenni and her brother Lupillo often talked about their experience selling cassettes at their father's stand at the Paramount

Swap Meet, about ten miles north of Long Beach. The whole family would go along to help their father. In those years, Jenni developed a real appreciation for Mexican music. She had been raised on a solid diet of the best mariachi and banda. But at the flea market, as she worked she put on the music that drew her the most, female artists like Rocio Durcal, Lupita D'Alessio and Isabel Pantoja, grand divas that would influence her own style later on.

Pedro and his children first started to learn the music business at the swap meet. For Pedro, it was where it all started. His business was gradually becoming more and more legitimate, more real, more viable. Now it wasn't just a pipe dream, he could make money with his passion.

Of course, thousands of people dream about making it in the music business, and work very hard to achieve it. In Pedro Rivera's case, it wasn't just hard work and passion. Aside from those two essential ingredients, Pedro had a natural business sense, and a nose for what could be really successful. The desire to produce and promote his own music and that of other artists who he believed in led him to form Cintas Acuario. But once his little business was launched, he also made several decisions that would prove critical to his success.

Pedro already knew he could make money selling cassettes, and later CDs. He had done it as a nightclub photographer, and he had done it at his little flea market table. But at the beginning, the artists came to him with a recording that they would give to him in exchange for him selling it. Pedro quickly realized that the real business was in owning the recordings, and not just promoting and selling them. Years later, his famous children would adopt the same philosophy: although both Jenni and Lupillo would eventually sign record contracts with major labels, they never ceded ownership of their recordings; they licensed rights to the labels for sales and promotion of the recordings.

The crucial decision to his success was recognizing and choosing which artists to work with, and which songs to record. When Pedro began his label, regional Mexican music, as it is known in the United States, was the top-selling genre of Latin music in the country. But "commercial" regional Mexican music, which got radio play, was mostly mariachi, norteña music in the vein of Los Tigres del Norte, or groups playing romantic music like Conjunto Primavera and Los Bukis. Pedro worked with artists like Graciela Beltran—who would go on to become one of the most important female mariachi singers in the country—and with el Chapo de Sinaloa. But he also discovered an overlooked subgenre: the corrido, and within that genre, the narcocorrido.

"I never could have gotten on the radio," Pedro said in a 2009 *Billboard* interview. "And that's why I said to my artists at the time: 'we have to study corridos, sing corridos, because corridos can help us to sell music even though we don't know how to sing. Many people buy corridos just for the stories they tell, not for who's singing them.'"

One of the first artists Pedro would record corridos with was Chalino Sanchez, a young singer-songwriter from Sinaloa who would become a legend after he was murdered in Mexico in 1992, at only thirty-two. Sanchez wrote and performed corridos with dark themes, alluding to narcotrafficking and violence. He got his start as a singer writing corridos commissioned by various people, including narcotraffickers.

Sanchez possessed certain qualities that Pedro appreciated as a musician: he wasn't a great singer, but he had a very distinctive, instantly recognizable voice; he sang corridos about things that had happened in real life; and he was totally genuine. There was nothing manufactured about Chalino Sanchez; he was a man of the people, for the people. And because he was so down-to-earth, he really connected with audiences. At the time, Pedro still held onto his own dreams of stardom. But as he saw how the careers of the artists on his record label took off, he realized that maybe it wasn't his moment, and that for now at least, he should focus on helping to launch the careers of others.

"In those years I made a decision," Pedro told *Billboard* in 2009, and then shared an anecdote he would retell in many interviews. "When I took Chalino and Graciela to a rodeo in Fresno, I saw how much energy they had. And I said to myself, 'what am I doing here with them,' because it was the three of us. And I thought, I'm either a singer, or I'm a producer. And I decided to be the producer."

Pedro Rivera would become perhaps the best-known and most influential producer of corridos of his generation. And the more he grew as a businessman, the more he involved his children in the business. Jenni was a key member of the team. By this point she had already studied business administration, she was very good with numbers, and great with people, and she could help out in different areas.

Few people on the outside really understand the complexities and challenges of the record business. Its main essence is discovering new talent, something Pedro did almost instinctively; he had a gift for recognizing the songs and unique voices that would grab people's attention. But what comes after is just as important. Pedro founded Cintas Acuario, with his own recording studio, so that he could have control over the artistic process, from beginning to end. He himself hired engineers, producers and musicians, and recorded in his own studio. He hired photographers, and he designed the album covers himself. And when it came time to sell the records, he began licensing his recordings to major record labels which typically pay an advance and/or royalties for the rights to commercially exploit a recording. But Pedro was the owner of the recordings, and that was key, because if he worked to develop an artist, and that artist only achieved success years later, then he could put out a compilation of their songs and sell it.

"The record label started to grow, and it surprised everyone," Jenni recalled in an interview with Susana Heredia for *TVNotas*. "I was selling real estate and Lupillo was working in restaurants. But it started to grow and my dad asked us to help out, and my brothers and I started to work more for him."

Throughout her years as a student, and later when she was a real estate agent, Jenni was also involved in every aspect of the record label. She and her brothers, as they themselves would describe it, did a little bit of everything: they were drivers; prepared contracts for artists and musicians; designed album covers; took pictures; packed up records; took orders; collected payments; handled distribution; and even handled promotion, limited as it may have been for a small independent label. That experience would prove to be formative later, for Jenni the artist.

By the time she was ready to completely focus on music, she knew the ins and outs of the business as well or even better than many label executives.

"I was the singer, and my children helped me," Pedro said in his interview with Octavio Acosta. "Sometimes I took them along to watch, for voice lessons, and I didn't know that they liked what I was doing. And then one day I hire a band to record and the singer didn't show up, and they used Lupillo to sing on the recording. And that was his first record. And he said to me, 'Papa, I recorded!' and I said, 'So take a picture and put out the record.'"

By then Lupillo was working full-time at Cintas Acuario, something Jenni never did, since she was doing very well selling real estate. Lupillo, on the other hand, had never gone to college. He worked preparing tacos and burritos in a restaurant until Pedro, who needed help with his label that was getting bigger by the day, asked his son to come work for him full-time.

Pedro asked his son how much they were paying him at the restaurant. When he said he made $195 a week, Pedro asked him, "If I pay more, will you come work for me?" And he offered Lupillo $250 a week. So Lupillo took the job at Cintas Acuario, and was put in charge of sales, managing the recording studio, and much more. "He learned a lot here," Pedro said in his interview with Acosta. "He learned what would sell, and what people liked." Those lessons would be key to his own success.

"There was a singer named Chavo Sanchez who sang really badly, and Lupillo said, 'I don't understand why he's so popular,'" Pedro recalled in the Octavio Acosta interview. "And on that record El Chavo had a corrido called 'El Moreno.' And Lupe said, 'Well I'm going to record that.' And he recorded 'El Moreno' and started promoting it in the north, and that was the hit."

As for Jenni, she hadn't sung since that contest at Long Beach when she had forgotten the words. She didn't sing in public again until 1993, when, separated from Trino, her girlfriends had invited her to go out for a few drinks. She had just ended an eight-year relationship that had begun when she was just fifteen, she had three children, and had spent practically her entire adolescence being a mother. She was only twenty-three, but she had lived enough for a forty-year-old.

"At the time I didn't know what a dance was, what going out was, I didn't know how to have fun," Jenni said at an interview for the 2012 *Billboard Latin Music Conference*, the annual convention for the Latin music industry held in Miami, where record labels, managers, radio executives, promoters and artists converge for three days of meetings and panels. "I was a mother going to high school and college. In 1993, at twenty-three I didn't know what the outside world was. My friends came over and said we're going out, you can't sit at home being depressed. And they took me to a dance club called El Rancho Grande in Carson, California. And that's where I found out what nightlife was, what it meant to go out, what tequila was, and that was the end of me. When they gave me a few tequila shots and got me half-drunk my friends dared me to get up on stage and sing, and I'm pretty buzzed and I say, 'Fine. You don't have to dare me, because I want to.'"

After years of not singing at all, years of following her mother's advice and studying for a career instead of following in her father's footsteps and pursuing music, she was ready to step out onto a different stage. And that night, after singing the Chalino Sanchez song, "Nieves de enero," as Jenni herself put it: "I liked the applause from the audience. Okay, it wasn't an audience. It was just a bunch of people as drunk as I was," she remembered, laughing. "Maybe they couldn't hear so good." But they did applaud, and that sparked an interest that she had never considered before.

Almost from the moment his first daughter was born, Pedro Rivera had wanted Jenni to be a singer. In 1993, at twenty-three, Jenni finally did as he wanted. Her career as a singer had begun.

CHAPTER 4

From Caterpillar to Butterfly

That night in 1993, when Jenni Rivera took the microphone at El Rancho Grande and sang "Nieves de enero," she took the first step toward a career in music. "Nieves de enero," a *ranchera* ballad by Chalino Sanchez about an impossible love, was very popular at the time, since Chalino had been murdered the year before, and all of his recordings had been rediscovered by an avid public. Of course Jenni had known Chalino, who had recorded for Cintas Acuario for a long time, and more than any other artist he had demonstrated the great commercial potential that corridos had.

The song Jenni sang that raucous night was a romantic ballad, not a corrido, and the crowd's positive, enthusiastic response propelled her to take her first steps as an artist. By that time, Cintas Acuario was a well-known, established, successful label with nice facilities. Jenni finally decided to make use of it, and give her father what he had always dreamed of: her record.

Jenni recorded an album of traditional songs with her brothers Pedro, Gustavo and Juan, and they called it *La Güera Rivera con banda*. The record didn't do much, but Jenni hadn't expected much either. From 1993 on, she recorded an album every year and gave it to her father, just because she wanted to, and because she knew it made him happy.

Meanwhile, Jenni kept on selling real estate and helping her father out at Cintas Acuario when she could. For his part, Pedro began building his daughter's catalog. Although nothing major had happened in her career as a singer, he knew it was only a matter of time. In 1994, Jenni repeated her formula of recording classic songs with her brothers with the album *Con los viajeros del norte*. These first few albums from Jenni featured photos of a young woman on the cover, with a contagious smile and rounded cheeks that made her look even younger than her twenty-three years. It's an open, warm face, of a friend, a confidante, the same charismatic face that would captivate her fans for the rest of her life. In those early years, the quick connection she made with her audience was obvious, even in 1995 when she donned a black cowboy hat, showing that from then on, this little girl was a force to be reckoned with.

I n 1995, regional Mexican music on the radio was an eclectic mix. It was dominated by Tejano artists like Selena, Michael Salgado and Mazz; and norteño groups like Los Tigres del Norte and Intocable, and romantic bands like Los Temerarios, Los Palominos and Bronco.

There wasn't a strong corrido presence on any commercial station. There were some groups like Los Tigres del Norte who sang narcocorridos, including the megahit "Camelia la tejana."

But the lyrics never captured the degree of detail and realism that Chalino Sanchez did, since he had lived through that kind of violence himself, and didn't mince words when he sang about it. So Chalino Sanchez never made any of the *Billboard* charts for radio hits. In her early days, Jenni Rivera didn't either. But by the mid-nineties, a major shift was taking place throughout Southern California, especially in Los Angeles. A new generation of Mexicans began to pop up in the media, in the entertainment world, and everywhere. They were children of immigrants, they spoke Spanish and English equally well, and celebrated their Mexican heritage, while adopting American customs and styles at the same time. These Mexicans drove around in lowriders (classic cars modified to drive lower to the ground than a regular car, and able to bounce up and down with the press of a button), listened to rap and hip-hop in English, and banda and mariachi music in Spanish, and wore baggy jeans with Mexican hats. The scene was a real cultural hybrid, just like Jenni, Lupillo, Juan and Gustavo Rivera themselves were.

Popular culture always takes its cues from street culture, and it was the same for the Rivera family, quintessential trendsetters. The corridos that Pedro Rivera promoted at Cintas Aquario and that Lupillo and Jenni were starting to sing were not played on the radio on the national level, but they were heard on the streets of Long Beach, Los Angeles and surrounding areas. Here, the new Latinos were very different from the Cuban Americans of Miami or the Puerto Ricans and Dominicans of New York City. In Southern California, the new Latin street culture was more closely tied to Mexican traditions, but at the same time was totally influenced by the populist, improvisational street culture of rap and hip-hop, with themes of violence and gangs resonating in both worlds.

In that environment, gradually, one record at a time, the Riveras started to make a name for themselves and developed a following.

CHAPTER 5

The Mother and First Lady
of Corrido

I n 1995, Jenni penned her first corrido, "La Chacalosa," a story rich in detail about the daughter of a drug trafficker who goes into the family business, selling the "best merchandise" the way her father taught her. It was a risky, surprising song, since up until then no women were writing or performing corridos of any kind, much less narcocorridos.

"I wrote it so I could be included along with all the men who sang corridos at the time. I was thinking of selling records, being different. So yes, of course there was criticism, but I think that was life teaching me I was going to be criticized but I'd still be standing anyway. And I've gone on like that ever since," Jenni emphasized on *Estudio Billboard* in 2010.

Jenni wanted to be different, and she succeeded. Ever since the beginning of the corrido tradition, women have been the subject of many songs, and many corridos tell of traffickers in a dress with a pistol. But those songs were almost always sung by a man, and even though a handful of women have sung narcocorridos—such as Dueto Amapola, Las Potranquitas and the popular "Alondra de la frontera" Lydia Mendoza—none of them were really able to make a career out of it.

Jenni Rivera wasn't the daughter of narcotraffickers, but she understood the world portrayed in the narcocorridos; after all, Cintas Acuario had released many records by Chalino Sanchez, El Chapo and Los Razos, some of the most popular corrido artists. In other words, Jenni had street cred.

And "La Chacalosa" worked because it sounded so real. When listeners heard verses about a girl who instead of having a lavish *quinceañera* party for her fifteenth birthday, was given a lucrative job in the family business, with a cell phone and a beeper, it wasn't hard to imagine that Jenni had really lived what she sang about in her strong, defiant voice. When at the end of the song she shouted out she'd see everyone again in Parral, El Farallon and La Sierra, she was talking about real places in Southern Californian where Chalino and El Chapo had sang, popular spots for corrido lovers. "Thanks to his album *En vivo desde El Farallon*, Chalino Sanchez put Los Angeles on the map as a new epicenter of corrido in the mid-nineties," explained Professor Jan Carlos Ramirez-Pimienta of San Diego State University, in an essay he wrote on the narcocorrido musical genre titled: "Sicarias, buchonas y jefes: perfiles de la mujer en el narcocorrido."

Jenni had not been closely touched by narco-violence as Chalino had, but she could sing those songs with authority. She came from the 'hood, from the streets. She knew about gangs, and working hard and not having anything to show for it, just like she understood the importance of family, honor, and moral codes. And at a time when female performers were women with pretty faces and slender figures, singing sweet songs about love and heartbreak, Jenni was real. With her open gaze, easy smile, and full curves, there was nothing artificial about her; she was your friend, your cousin, your sister. When she said to her sisters from the tough L.A. streets that her fifteenth birthday present hadn't been a *quinceñera* or "sweet fifteen" party but a shady business and a beeper, the message was irresistibly illicit. And in the United States, where Mexican teens had more freedom, that message could be delivered with a female voice; of course, as Jenni said herself, the harsh criticism was inevitable, but at the same time, she found an avid audience.

So avid that Jenni started being known as "the first lady of corrido," and the major record label Sony Records licensed her album *Reina de Reinas*, a collection of songs within the corrido genre, many written by Jenni herself.

The album was so well received that her songs started getting some airplay on local radio stations. One key player that helped Jenni get on the radio was La Que Buena (KBUE), a Mexican music station that really took off in 1995 and played what other commercial stations wouldn't touch: corridos, narcocorridos and new artists. So La Que Buena and its program director, Pepe Garza, were among the first to support Jenni Rivera and her music.

Garza recalled during a television interview that it had been Jenni's father, Pedro Rivera, who first presented her music to him. But at that time, they had really been pushing Lupillo, who with his deep voice stood out from all the other corrido singers trying to imitate the late Chalino Sanchez. But one day, dropping by the station, "Pedro Rivera gave me a record and said, 'See, my daughter sings too.' And I liked it," Garza remembered. "I had my doubts at the beginning, because women don't have much luck in regional Mexican music. But she started to win over the audience."

Meanwhile, Jenni kept on working selling real estate. After all, she had three children to raise, and she was still very far from making a living just through music . . . until her songs started getting radio play.

"And in 1999, in Compton, California, while I was driving some clients to show them a house, I heard my music on the radio on KBUE in Los Angeles," Jenni said in an interview at the *Billboard Latin Music Conference* in April 2012. What she heard that day was "Reina de reinas," a corrido written by Vicente Estrada that tells the story of a narcotrafficker. It starts off, *I'm the queen of queens, from Jalisco/ my crown is white, of what they call perico* (cocaine)/ *And I bring it along everywhere, I don't take any chances.*

"I had a Pontiac and the engine would overheat, and when that song came on the radio, my clients were outside pushing the car, because it was stalled in the middle of the street," Jenni recalled. "And I was driving and I had the radio on, and that's when I heard my song."

When thousands of people started listening to Jenni's songs every day on the radio, her musical career got to the next level. She was still selling real estate. As Garza remembered, "One time I got Jenni and Graciela Beltran together for an interview, and Graciela said to her, 'the last time I saw you, you were selling me a house!'" But once her music started to be heard, and more importantly, once she realized she liked it, things changed.

"Soon local nightclubs started calling me, asking me to come out and sing," she said in the interview. "And they said they would pay me, I don't know, fifty, sixty, seventy dollars to sing a few songs. And I thought, 'with that money I could buy some beans, some rice, some tortillas, some food for dinner, and go out and have a little fun.' And that's when I got more seriously interested, and I thought, 'fine, I'll do this for a couple of years,' and here I am, I've been singing ever since 1999." And that's how she changed careers.

CHAPTER
6

Love Is All I Know

In hindsight, one may wonder why Jenni didn't devote herself to music full-time much sooner, given that she had all the key ingredients to pursue it: the voice, the record label, musicians, her father, credibility. But Jenni was a multifaceted woman. On the one hand, she was an educated businesswoman, and she had other options. On the other hand, she was a mother, and her children were always her first priority. She was not going to pursue anything that wouldn't allow her to take good care of them.

And Jenni was a woman who wanted love. But in that area, she didn't seem to have the best luck. Her relationship with her first husband, Trino, had been painful and problematic. Now, in the early nineties, Jenni had three children she was raising all on her own. It was an incredibly hard job, and, no doubt, a father for them would have been very welcome.

In 1995, Jenni met a man who seemed to be just perfect. One night, while out singing in a bar, she fell in love. Things started off great. In a 2003 interview with *La Opinion*, Jenni said that when she met Juan Lopez it was love at first sight. "Juan and I met on February 25, 1995, in El Farallon, in Lynwood," Jenni remembered. "I was there to see a friend of mine sing. I wasn't going to sing, but somebody asked me to get up and sing 'La Chacalosa.' So I got up on stage, and that's when Juan noticed I was there."

Lopez knew who Jenni was, and he took the opportunity to have a picture taken with her. But that wasn't enough. When the show was over, he waited for her out in the parking lot, and asked her to have dinner with him. Jenni said no, but she did give him her phone number.

They started dating. But not long after, federal authorities arrested Lopez, charging him with trafficking illegal immigrants into the United States, and he was sentenced to six months in prison. Then Jenni's musical career was just beginning to take off, as she continued selling real estate and recorded albums on the side. When Lopez was released in 1997, Jenni started dating him again, and soon she was pregnant. Jenni was in love, and she was happy. On June 9, 1997, Jenni Rivera married Juan Lopez, both deeply in love with each other. On October 3 of that year, their daughter Jenicka Priscilla Lopez was born.

Everything seemed to go along smoothly. But less than a year after they were married, her husband was unfaithful to her, and they separated. Still Jenni longed for a stable family for her children, and she decided to give their marriage another chance.

Jenni was in love with Juan, but she admitted in an interview with *La Opinion* that the problems between them began to surface after they had been dating for just three months. In spite of this, they were so in love they decided to stay together and get married.

"We couldn't stay away from each other, in spite of our problems," Jenni said in the interview. "We both forgave each other for many things because of the real affection we felt, and I always thought we could make it better. I fought hard for my marriage, and I wanted it to work."

From 1999 on, her career began to grow. And with all that came with it, Jenni managed to balance her three roles as wife, mother, and developing artist. She did this for a few years, and on February 11, 2001, she had her fifth and last child, a son, Johnny Angel Lopez. And then her marriage really started to fall apart.

CHAPTER

7

The Hardest Test

Nineteen ninety-seven was a big year for Jenni Rivera. She was in love with Juan Lopez, and together they were expecting a baby girl. Her musical career was on the rise; her fame grew with each passing day. But in the middle of this happiness, Jenni had to face what would perhaps be the greatest test of her life. That same year, she found out that Trino, her first husband and father of her three eldest children, had sexually abused her younger sister Rosie. And later, to her absolute horror, she discovered he had also abused their own daughter, Chiquis.

"When I found out in 1997 that the father of my children had done that, I wanted to kill him," Jenni said in a television interview with Susana Heredia on *TVNotas*. "I wanted to beat him to death since I didn't have a gun. But I was pregnant with Jenicka. So I couldn't do anything but wait. My daughter was born a little premature, because of the stress, the hormones."

Sexual abuse is a taboo subject everywhere, especially in traditional Latin cultures steeped in machismo. For Rivera, admitting and dealing with what had happened was devastating, but necessary. The steady courage she showed in speaking publicly about something so personal and so painful for her closest loved ones would also come to define the artist and persona she would eventually become. Jenni never tried to avoid any question, controversy, rumor or accusation. After confronting head-on one of the hardest things a person could ever have to face—especially a mother—Jenni wasn't afraid of anything. Jenni not only faced what had happened, she spoke about it publicly, and did whatever she could to make sure the abuser was brought to justice. As soon as she found out about what had happened, and in spite of the fact that the abuse had taken place years before, she went to the authorities immediately and filed a restraining order so that Trino could not come near her children. The next step was to have police arrest her ex-husband, who had disappeared as soon as he heard about charges being filed against him. It would take almost ten years to locate Trino, have him arrested, and bring him to trial. Jenni did not rest until her mission was finally accomplished.

Someone once asked her how she found the courage to continue her Don Quixote–like quest, and she responded frankly: "The truth is a person that does that kind of damage to kids doesn't just do it one time. And I was doing research during those nine years that he was a fugitive. I studied the characteristics of people who abuse children. They are sick people, they can't control themselves. I felt it was my responsibility if I had gone through it, and that my children and my sister were more or less getting past it. We had to be an example. Especially with such a taboo subject that no one talks about. It happens a lot. It's very sad."

Over the years, Jenni, Rosie, and to a lesser degree, Chiquis all openly talked about the abuse they had suffered from Trino. They often said they talked about it publicly in order to help other women who could be going through something similar. In one particularly detailed interview, the three women and Jacquis talked about it with Charytin, the host of *Escándalo TV*. Jenni described how she had discovered that Trino had abused her daughter and little sister.

"This is the hardest thing I've ever gone through in my life," Jenni said. "We had been separated for five years by then, and for five years he had visited my daughter on the weekends. I had a feeling, and I told Rosie, I had a feeling something wasn't right, and I asked her."

Rosie, Jenni's little sister who she adored with all her heart, was sexually abused by Trino beginning when she was seven and continuing until she was eleven years old. Born in 1981, Rosie was much younger than Jenni, and, of course, much more vulnerable.

Years later, in an effort to overcome what had happened to her, Rosie turned to Bible study and the word of God. Today she often speaks about her experience, and how to forgive and move on.

"I thought I had to keep it a secret," she said in one speech she gave in 2011, which was videotaped and posted on YouTube in October 2012. The description posted says "She talks about how sexual abuse at the age of seven left her crippled like Mephibosheth in the Bible. After eighteen years of suffering, depression and trauma for fear no one would ever want to marry her, God redeems her and gives her a princess wedding. See the photos while listening to one abused girl's story. God can also give back to you everything that has been stolen."

In Rosie's testimonial, divided in two different videos, her eloquent voice is heard while a slideshow displays preparations for her wedding. Rosie begins her presentation asking the audience to read a passage from the Bible, and then she talks about her own experience as a survivor of sexual abuse, recalling how she felt when she was just a terrified little girl.

"A nine-year-old girl thought she had to save her sister's life," she said. "When he abused me, that man threatened that if I told anyone, he was going to kill my sister. My sister was my hero, my best friend, she was everything I wanted to be."

That's why Rosie did not say a word for several years, until she was eleven and the abuse stopped. By then Jenni had separated from Trino, and he had started abusing his own daughter, Chiquis.

"After he and Jenni separated, he kept on doing the same thing to Chiquis. I could tell that Chiquis hated him, and I didn't know why. Then I found out he was doing the same thing to her that he did to me," Rosie said in the interview with *Escándalo TV*.

If Rosie was afraid to talk about the abuse she suffered, Chiquis, who was even smaller, was completely terrified. After all, Trino was her own father. Chiquis told *Escándalo TV* that at the beginning, she didn't understand what was happening.

"I didn't know that it was bad until they started to teach us about sex at school, and then I understood," she said. "During the day," her father was "very caring, very playful." But at night she was afraid of him.

Telling her mother seemed impossible. When Charytin asked on *Escándalo TV* why she hadn't told Jenni sooner, Chiquis replied, "Because I know her, and I knew she would kill him. Then I thought, what am I going to do with my mom in jail, and my dad dead? Who would I end up with?"

For Jenni, the discovery was devastating. Her life revolved around her family, especially her children and her sister, who was like a daughter to her. At first, she didn't have the healthiest reaction, and, as she admitted on *Escándalo TV*, even contemplated suicide for the second time in her life.

"My sister was the light of my life, and I felt guilty for what had happened," Jenni explained. "Later I find out that he did it to my daughters too, the doctor tells me he did it to the little one Jackeline since she was four years old, really little. She blocked it from her mind. I couldn't sleep. I sat on the couch with a knife, waiting for him."

In spite of the trauma she was going through, Jenni did not stand idly by. She went to the police and formally accused Trino of sexually abusing her daughters and sister. But before Trino could be brought in for questioning, he fled, becoming a fugitive of justice. It would be years before he was captured and went to trial, but in the meantime, Jenni and her family began the arduous journey of processing what had happened and moving past it.

When Charytin asked Chiquis what advice she would give to sexual abuse victims, she offered a clear answer: "Tell someone, you don't know how liberated you'll feel. Do it to help other people who are going through the same thing."

What Jenni suffered at Trino's hands affected her for the rest of her life, in a thousand different ways. She grew even stronger, more determined than ever, and more protective of her family. Her children have always been at the center of her world, and knowing how deeply they had been hurt gave her a new purpose, and a new responsibility. Nothing like that would happen again, ever. Over the years, Jenni talked openly many times about what it meant to be a survivor of abuse, and the experience inspired her to found the Jenni Rivera Love Foundation in 2005, created to help families and women who had been abused.

But just as her personal life shattered into a million pieces, her musical career continued to get bigger. And everything that she went through—her loves, breakups, tragedies, challenges, her grudges, revenges, triumphs, her joys, everything—Jenni poured into her records and songs. She was, as she put it herself, an open book.

CHAPTER 8

The Warrior Butterfly Is Born

In 1999, while she was sorting through the fallout from Trino, and separating from and then reconciling with Juan Lopez, Rivera signed a record contract—a licensing deal, as usual—with Fonovisa, the leading label for regional Mexican music in the United States. Her first album for that deal was *Que me entierren con la banda*, and featured several songs Jenni had written: "Que un rayo te parta," "Solo sé amor," and what would be the album's first single release, "Las Malandrinas."

According to Professor Juan Carlos Ramirez-Pimienta of San Diego State University, "Las Malandrinas" ("bad girls") was written for Mexican women in the United States who like popular culture, and the lyrics reflect that. She sings, "They call us malandrinas because we're loud, we drink beer, we like the best wine, at the dance clubs we always ask for corridos . . . we're not afraid of anything." And when it came to men, "we like really well-dressed guys, with their cowboy boots, classy and strong, who don't disappear when the check comes along . . ."

The lyrics of the song are fun and exactly what young Latinas, so underrepresented in popular culture, would identify with. But the video for "Las Malandrinas" is very raw. Directed by Danny Suarez, and produced on a shoestring budget by Pedro Rivera for his Cintas Acuario label, it could be a video for urban music, for a gritty song about life in the 'hood —but featuring young Mexican girls from the streets of Los Angeles who drink, shoplift CDs from record stores, party hard, and beat up las "Popis," the well-dressed, well-behaved "good" girls. At one point, outside the record store the girls have just been shoplifting in, the Malandrinas grab one of the Popis, tie her hands and legs, gag her, and throw her into the trunk of a car, headed to a party. Aside from the video's content, which stirred up quite a controversy on television shows, the Malandrinas were not your typical pretty models, which are generally the only kind of women ever featured in music videos. These were clearly real girls from the barrio, of all shapes, colors and sizes, dressed in cheap clothes, with tattoos and heavy makeup.

"Las Malandrinas are the 'bad girls' but not in the bad sense of the word, or in a negative way," Jenni told *Billboard* in 2012. "I wrote it as an homage to my women fans. To the girls who go out to the clubs, who drink tequila and take care of themselves. The song blew up. People were interested. At that moment Jenni Rivera was really born as an artist. Because there's no better way to get attention than to get to women. I am a woman. I understand how we are. There are more women in this world than men, and I always thought they were my market. They are the consumers, and they're the people who understand me. That's why I've kept on writing songs like that."

Now, remember what the music scene was like in 1999 and

2000. The biggest female artists were Thalia, Paulina Rubio, Jennifer Lopez, Shakira, and Pilar Montenegro. Their videos were designed to capitalize on the considerable sex appeal those women had. In regional Mexican music, there were few big female stars at all, and they looked nothing like Jenni: Graciela Beltran, Jennifer Peña, Ana Gabriel, and, just outside of that orbit, Paquíta la del Barrio. No matter where you looked, Jenni Rivera and her music may as well have been from another planet.

But to the many Mexican American women in and around Los Angeles, Jenni Rivera was definitely not from another planet. On the contrary, she was the first artist they'd ever seen who looked like them. A large group of women saw a reflection of themselves in Jenni Rivera, just as so many Mexican American girls had seen themselves in Selena ten years before. Still, Jenni had several challenges ahead of her. As Pepe Garza observed, in the world of regional Mexican music, female artists were rare, and still are. But Jenni had a crucial stroke of luck: she signed with Fonovisa, a label that saw in her the same thing her growing fan base saw. Jenni began releasing records with them in 2000, and never left (although she never relinquished ownership of her masters).

"I signed with Fonovisa for the first time in 2000 because the other labels weren't interested in promoting my music, and they didn't see any future for me as an artist," Jenni said a few years ago, when her label was celebrating its twenty-fifth year in business. "I brought 'Las Malandrinas' to them, and they believed in me." Fonovisa had vision, Jenni added. "They see beyond the present. They think about what we artists can give in the future, and how we can grow and evolve as artists."

Fonovisa was and still is the biggest label for regional Mexican music, with artists such as Los Tigres del Norte, Marco Antonio Solis and Banda El Recodo on their roster. They had female artists too, but none that remotely resembled Jenni Rivera, starting with the fact that Jenni sang corridos. They saw a totally new kind of artist in Jenni, she was different, vibrant and emotional. They saw possibilities.

On the day she died at the height of her fame, ironically, the characteristics that had at one time caused some to doubt her chances of success were the very same elements that her record label now praised.

"The fact that Jenni was born in the United States to illegal immigrant parents is very significant in terms of having a career from that background," Victor Gonzalez, President of Universal Music Latin Entertainment, the record company that includes Fonovisa, said to *Billboard* after Jenni's death. "Being a woman, always holding onto her family values, always protecting her own, creates a very specific profile of many people, many women, many mothers who have gone through similar experiences. And it's transcendent."

Today, when we look back on Jenni's life, and look forward to her legacy, we realize how universal those aspects of her story were. But when Jenni was just starting out, things weren't so clear. Making the decision to not try and hide who she was but instead to celebrate her identity and publicly confront her problems and challenges meant taking a big risk. But from adversity comes strength. If she had not had to face such adversity, she may never have reached the level of stardom that she did.

"I didn't decide to really be a singer until I heard so many people in the industry criticizing what I wanted to do. I didn't want to do anything. Recording music was just a hobby," Jenni said in her interview at the *Billboard* conference in April 2012. "When I heard so much negativity, that a single mom, and a woman with Jenni Rivera's body, that she couldn't amount to anything in music. At that time and now—but more back then because they saw they lost a lot of money—the record companies manufactured artists. They would find pretty girls in the street and tell them: 'You're going to record this and learn this by heart.' That's why they didn't sell. But they spent $80,000 on a video. But I wasn't that manufactured artist. I was a real woman singing about what I lived. And the women listening to me on the radio or on the records we sold at the flea markets lived the same things that I did, and that was the connection. That's why I kept singing. Just to show them I could do it. I thought I would just do it for two years, and that was the biggest lie because now I've spent fifteen years at it."

CHAPTER 9

Road to Stardom

The year 2001 was an extraordinary year for Jenni Rivera. After a brief separation from her husband Juan Lopez, she had gotten back together with him, and on February 11 their son, Johnny Angel Lopez was born.

At the same time, Jenni's musical career was really getting off the ground. Although the media still referred to her as "Lupillo Rivera's sister"—since her brother was an established artist whose records with Sony were flying off the shelves—it was clear that Jenni also had the potential to reach great heights. Curiosity about this fledgling artist grew, and the media speculated about her family, her background, her supposed rivalry with Lupillo (which did not exist; Lupillo and Jenni always had an extremely close relationship), and her love life. At thirty-one, Jenni knew how to handle herself in the face of rising scrutiny. She started to realize that no matter what she did or said, somebody, somewhere was going to have an opinion about it, and she was ready to confront those opinions.

The first Jenni Rivera song to appear on the *Billboard* charts was "Querida socia" in April 2001. It was a banda song, with a full brass section and accordion, with decidedly controversial lyrics. It told the story of two women sharing the same man; one the "good" girl who he is going to marry, while Jenni sings from the point of view of the other woman, who plans to continue her red-hot affair with her lover even after he's married. In one provocative line, Jenni sings: "You can keep that wedding dress, and I'll keep the bed/ just one last thing: you wash his clothes, and I'll take them off."

"Querida Socia" was written by Manuel Eduardo Toscano, the songwriter from Veracruz, Mexico who was known as a real hit maker in regional Mexican music, regularly penning songs for such artists as Vicente Fernandez and Los Tigres del Norte. Toscano was also the principal composer for Paquíta la del Barrio. He had a clear understanding of what songs would be popular with a female audience. "Querida Socia" was perfect for Jenni, since she put herself in the role of so many "other women," while the song also struck a chord for many others who had been cheated on themselves.

Jenni sang it with a sense of humor and panache, and when she talked about it she took the same approach, demonstrating that after ten years she knew how to work the media very well. When the magazine *La Revista Perrona* interviewed her in March 2001, for example, she was asked who she represented in the song: the woman washing the man's clothes, or the woman peeling them off.

"Ah man, it's great, isn't it? I think every woman could be a little of both, if she wants. Being the other woman isn't very good exactly, but I think you feel even worse sitting home like an idiot washing his clothes while the guy goes with the other woman and she takes them off! I'd rather take them off!!"

"Querida socia" was the first single off of *Déjate amar*, Jenni's debut album with Fonovisa. Its release coincided with the birth of her younger son, Johnny Angel Lopez. The close timing of the two events meant that Jenni could not promote the album full-out. Still, on April 21, 2001, "Querida socia" debuted on *Billboard*'s Regional Mexican Airplay chart, which ranks songs according to how many times they are played on regional Mexican music stations all across the country. "Querida socia" entered at number 25, and a week later reached its highest position at number 18.

It stayed on the chart for eighteen weeks. For its part, *Déjate amar* never appeared on any *Billboard* charts, partly because Jenni could not do as much promotion as she would have had she not just given birth to her son. Nevertheless, Jenni was on the music industry's radar, so much so that *Billboard* reviewed the album upon its release, suggesting that Jenni had a very bright future ahead of her:

Déjate amar
Jenni Rivera
Producer: Pedro Rivera
Fonovisa FPCD10125

On her major-label debut, Jenni Rivera (Lupillo's sister) takes her brother's route and sings with banda, adapting rancheras and corridos to the format. Rivera's powerful yet subtle voice provides a good balance for the rough banda accompaniment, even on such tunes as "Agente de Ventas," a corrido about drug dealers penned by Lupillo. At the same time, Rivera has the spirit and personality to bring alive such tunes as "Querida Socia," a letter from a gloating mistress to a wife, and the versatility to carry off Freddie Fender's "Wasted Days and Wasted Nights" in English.

—L.C.

Déjate amar was in fact not her major-label debut; she put out her second album with Fonovisa after launching another record with Sony. But it was the album that firmly established Jenni as an artist. With *Déjate amar*, Jenni not only began to get more radio play, she also started to forge her musical identity. She was still basically a local or regional artist, with a fan base concentrated in California, but her potential on the national and international stage was taking shape.

Outside of music, it's impressive to see the level of clarity and self-assuredness Jenni possessed in terms of defining her identity, her place in the musical landscape, and her goals for the future. In 2001, Jenni was thirty-one, the mother of five, and was certainly no naïve little girl. But few artists are able to maintain such clearly defined, consistent outlooks over the course of their careers. It's common to look back over an artist's career and see inconsistencies in what they have said over the years. But with Jenni, it was the opposite: it didn't matter what anyone else said about her, or how much she was criticized, her positions and opinions never wavered. And she never changed her story about where she came from, and where she was headed.

"Any human being can work really hard to be successful, but

that doesn't mean you forget that you were poor," she said in an interview with the magazine *El Aviso*, published in 2001. "Real riches are in your feelings, and that gets projected into what you accomplish. The real achievement in life is being able to identify with your people, with the community you're a part of," Jenni emphasized.

While she was promoting *Déjate amar*, in one of the first big articles written about Jenni, published in *La Opinion*, the veteran journalist Ramón Inclan described the singer as "possessing a strong, defiant voice, with songs of love for men, and against them. In her interpretative style, Jenni Rivera is a combination of Lupita D'Alessio and Paquíta la del Barrio, with a voice reminiscent of Chayito Valdez (although more powerful)."

Jenni no doubt appreciated these kinds of descriptions. And, with good reason, she was very offended by offhanded media coverage claiming her success and the success of her whole family was due to nothing more than a stroke of luck, or that she and Lupillo were locked in a bitter rivalry.

"To Lupillo and me, as artists, it's very painful to hear stories about us saying we've gotten to where we are out of sheer luck," Jenni told *La Opinion*. "The Riveras are not successful by magic, or because we illegally sell I don't know what. Just the opposite; not only are we not narcotraffickers, we're a very determined family, who our father, Don Pedro Rivera, raised to be honorable, humble and hardworking."

As far as her supposed rivalry with Lupillo, Jenni was unequivocal: "There's always plenty of negative people who want to cause conflicts. But trying to do that with us always fails because we're a very unified family, we help each another. For me, anything good that happens to Lupillo makes me really happy, because he's my brother and I love him, and I know how hard he's struggled to get to where he is. And I think he feels the same way for me."

No matter whatever negative commentaries were circulating in the media, the truth is that 2001 was a very good year for Jenni. Her son was born, who she adored. She released her second album with Fonovisa, and it was a success. Her marriage to Juan Lopez was solid. In fact, Juan was at her side the whole time during the *La Opinion* interview, something that Ramón Inclan made a note of in his article: "While we talked, Jenni Rivera's husband, Juan Lopez, did not leave her side for a minute. As Jenni puts it, Juan is a good man, and when they met, Cupid's arrow hit its target."

Although Jenni and Juan had had their ups and downs, they seemed to have worked out their problems. At least from the outside they seemed to be more in love than ever, and Juan was showing that he could be an understanding husband, fully supportive of her success. That kind of support from her partner was extremely important to a woman like Jenni, who so highly valued her independence, and her work.

"Honestly I believe women have the same rights as men in everything, including in love," Jenni said in her interview with *El Aviso*. "Love is a generous, sublime feeling, and it needs to be mirrored in both partners; I could talk about this a great deal because my husband and I have a great friendship, he supports me unconditionally, and in him I can find every reason to succeed. I'm a defender of women's rights, because if I can open someone's eyes through my songs, then I've done my part," she said.

Aside from the success she was achieving in record sales and radio play, Jenni was becoming a sought-after live performer. The offers to perform came from all over, including from families with ties to narcotrafficking who wanted to hire Jenni to perform at their daughters' *quinceañera* parties. She turned down these offers as graciously as she could so as not to offend anyone, saying there was simply no available time in her schedule.

Jenni and her brothers had one strict policy: they did not perform at private events. It was a rule Jenni said she followed to the end. In September 2012, mere months before her death and ten years after her career began to take flight, she said almost the exact same thing when a reporter from *La Opinion* asked her if she ever performed at private parties: "No, I don't need to," she said. "Look what a scare Ramon Ayala had, and he's a legend. Who needs that? It's true that sometimes you just don't know [exactly who's hiring you]."

Jenni was referring to a story that was widely publicized in 2009: Ramon Ayala had been performing at a private party held on an estate, when Mexican naval forces raided the property and arrested him along with some others. It turned out the hosts of the party were narcotraffickers, although Ayala said he did not know who the owners of the home were, or who was throwing the party.

"They tell you, 'You're going to perform at such and such a place, and you'll get paid this much,'" Jenni continued. "I said, 'No, I don't want any trouble.' And it's too bad, because there are some people with a lot of money who could afford to pay for a Jenni concert. But it's better not to take the risk."

Ten years earlier, Jenni hadn't taken the risk either. And she hadn't needed to. The more her music was heard, the more she was asked to perform live at all kinds of events and nightclubs. So Jenni started earning some serious money, enough to buy a new house in Corona, an hour away from Long Beach. It was one of the most important achievements of her early musical career, since Jenni had particularly painful memories of living in an unheated garage with her four-year-old daughter years before. Now, she finally felt like she was on solid ground, financially and emotionally. And she had a house worthy of her children, something Jenni described as "a great personal achievement, especially when my oldest daughter said, 'Thanks mom, because this is a great house, nothing like that garage we lived in.'"

CHAPTER
10

Family Ties

In the first years of the new millennium, Jenni started blossoming into a real star. It was a process that to some seemed to have taken place overnight, but nothing could have been further from the truth. With few exceptions, the road to stardom is a very long one, paved with tremendous amounts of hard work and sacrifice. The journey is made up of countless small steps, taken one after another, over the course of several years: an interview here, a show there, spending many hours on the road driving to visit countless little radio stations, spread all over the map, visits to record stores who are really not interested in your product, records put out with no marketing support, singles released that never make it onto the radio.

That Jenni had to make that same arduous journey, and that it took years before she earned any kind of serious recognition, is not at all unusual. The stories of other big names in the genre, such as Vicente Fernandez, Paquíta la del Barrio, Los Tigres del Norte, Intocable, and Selena herself, are stories of endless perseverance; they are stories of people who insist on succeeding in

spite of the formidable obstacles in their path, people who dog-
gedly keep on moving ahead, no matter how many times they
hear the word "no."

Jenni's circumstances were even more challenging than those
of most artists. It wasn't just that she was a woman trying to be a
singer in a male-dominated genre; she was from a poor background, the mother of five children, coming from an abusive
relationship, and even though she was pretty and outgoing, her
full figure did not fit the stereotype of the thin, model-perfect
body most female music stars seemed to have as a prerequisite to
success. And, as a corrido singer, working in a very macho, male-
dominated field where women were not always respected, she
had her share of ugly experiences.

Years later, in a May 2011, television interview on *Casa
Adelita*, Pedro Rivera recalled that one time, after she had barely
started singing, Jenni told him she was going to quit. The reason? She and her band had been hired to perform at the Carna-
val de Ensenada. But the man who had hired them, a friend of
Pedro Rivera's, wanted Jenni to perform certain other favors for
him, before he would pay her.

"My daughter went, she sang, and the reason she wanted to
quit is because my friend who had hired her wanted her to sleep
with him before he would pay her the $300 [that he had agreed
to pay]," Pedro said, his eyes welling with tears. "And I said,
'that's okay, daughter. You can stop. But just do one last record,
like I want.' And that's when I convinced her to sing corridos."

By 2002, the factors that had worked against Jenni were now
working in her favor. Singing corridos would give her a space in
the marketplace. Being full-figured and curvy would let her fe-

male audience easily identify with her, and the fact that she was a mother and had come out of an abusive relationship only strengthened their identification with her. And aside from all of that, Jenni had another incredibly powerful weapon in her arsenal. She was a member of the Rivera family.

At the beginning, when Jenni first started singing, the fact that she was Pedro's daughter clearly gave her a certain advantage, since her father had a recording studio, the know-how and the connections needed to record her and set her career in motion. Then came Lupillo's success. Like his sister, Lupillo had started off singing corridos for Cintas Acuario, and later, in 2001, he released *Despreciado* with Sony Music, and it was a major hit.

Despreciado is a collection of Mexican songs, some well-known, some brand-new, sung accompanied by a brass band in the Sinaloense style. This was all normal enough. But Lupillo himself, with his shaved head, the Bentley featured on his album covers, his expensive custom-tailored suits and his cigars, presented an image totally different from what had been associated with Mexican music up until then.

Despreciado was a sensation, selling over a million copies. The next album Lupillo released with Sony, *Sufriendo a solas*, also had sales that topped one million. At one point in 2002, Lupillo had four albums on *Billboard*'s chart for the Top 50 best-selling Latin albums in the country.

The mere fact that Jenni was Lupillo's sister was noteworthy in itself. There was no other well-known singer in Latin music who had a sibling who was also a singer (with the exception of brother-sister acts who performed together, like Pimpinela in Argentina and Jesse y Joy in Mexico). But aside from Lupillo, Gustavo, Juan and, to a lesser extent, Pedro Jr., also sang. The three brothers had varying degrees of success, and none reached the level of Lupillo or Jenni, but they had legitimate careers, and made their livings playing music. They sang, recorded records, and released singles. How many families had five siblings who were all recording artists? So Jenni attracted attention simply for being a part of her family. For many media outlets, especially in California, the story of the musical, talented Rivera family was irresistible.

And then there was the public's growing fascination for Jenni herself. She wasn't just a Rivera, she had a full, powerful voice in her own right. She was incredibly charismatic on stage, and on screen. She was beautiful, with a strong, effusive personality. And her songs connected with women everywhere. Watching the videos available on YouTube of Jenni from this time, the star power she already had shines through. It was only a matter of time before her fame would skyrocket, just like her brother's had.

In early 2002 Jenni traveled to Culiacan, Sinaloa to record her next album, which would be produced by her father. She would sing accompanied by the Banda Coyonqueños de Vicente Duarte.

Consistent with her image of a strong, independent woman that Jenni would develop, the album was titled *Se las voy a dar a otro* [I'm going to give it to someone else], which was also the title of the first single. The song chastises a man who doesn't know how to accept the love his woman offers him. Now, Jenni sang, "I'm going to give it to someone else/ because you don't deserve it/ you had it for so long/ and you didn't appreciate it/ you were busy doing whatever."

In the production of *Se las voy a dar a otro*, it's apparent that Jenni and her label were putting more effort—and more money—into her recordings. The album includes a wide range of styles—no corridos—including romantic songs, and even a song in English, "Angel Baby," also with traditional brass band accompaniment. It was such a unique sound that even though it was sung in English, "Angel Baby" hit *Billboard*'s Regional Mexican Airplay chart, remaining there for seven weeks and peaking at number 16.

There also began to be a steady stream of items about Jenni in the press. Stories described her as "Lupillo Rivera's controversial sister," to quote a piece from *La Prensa de San Diego* of that year, and as a sympathetic, homegrown singer.

To top it off, Jenni earned her first Grammy nomination with *Se las voy a dar a otro*, for Best Banda Album. Jenni had also been nominated for los Premios Que Buena, music awards that had begun in 2000 and were sponsored by JBUE-La Que Buena, the radio station that had thrown its support behind Jenni from the very beginning of her musical career. While los Premios Que Buena were specifically for Mexican music, the Latin Grammys were international in scope, and put Jenni on a whole new level. She was definitely not the little Mexican girl from Long Beach who sang provocative corridos anymore, she had managed to become a serious, respected artist.

It's very fitting that *Se las voy a dar a otro* is dedicated to what were and would always be the four pillars in Jenni's life: her family, her children, her work, and her fans. "We made this record with a lot of love for my wonderful fans who have supported me throughout my career, and who show me so much love at my shows," Jenni wrote. "This is dedicated to them and my brothers and sister, who I love so much and who always stay close to me on the phone, even if I'm far away working. To Gustavo, Lupillo, Pedro, Rosita and my little brother Juan, because even though you're grown, you'll always be my little boy. I'm so grateful to everyone who supports my music, everyone on my team and my parents, to my children who I miss so much because I have to leave them for work, which is so hard, but I love what I do, for what our generous audience gives back to us."

That September, Jenni attended her first Latin Grammys at the Kodak Theater in Los Angeles, wearing a low-cut black gown with a red floral pattern, and a sexy slit up one leg. The night before she had gone to the Person of the Year dinner in honor of Vicente Fernandez, and also wore another extremely low-cut black dress. She looked absolutely radiant, and for good reason. Even though she was just an hour away from the neighborhood she had grown up in, it was as if she had traveled light years away, to another galaxy. Jenni did not win a Grammy that year, but it was very clear that she had entered a new phase in her soaring career as an artist.

CHAPTER 11

Of Love and Other Demons

In 2003, Jenni's career took another turn. Instead of just re-cording another banda album, her next project was *Homenaje a las grandes,* a concept album in which she paid tribute to the greatest women of Latin music, reinterpreting their hits with banda arrangements, her unwavering voice accompanied by a brass band. The songs as well as their original singers held a great deal of meaning for Jenni, and many of them—Lupita D'Alessio, Lola Beltran, Rocio Durcal—were artists she had openly admired ever since she had first started singing. In *Homenaje a las grandes* Jenni also did cover versions of songs by Gloria Trevi ("Papa sin catsup") and Alejandra Guzman ("Hacer el amor con otro"), both artists who would become her friends, and who she would eventually perform on stage with. She also included a track in English, a cover of the Motown hit "Where Did Our Love Go," demonstrating once again her interest and love for the music in English that she had listened to so much as a child.

Beyond the music, the album marked a new direction in Jenni's look and aesthetic. After several album covers featuring Jenni in cowboy hats, here Jenni just wore a long, straight, strawberry blonde hair style against a white background. And instead of looking straight into the camera, as she always had before, her gaze is lowered, looking to the side, and her face looks slender. It's a decidedly timeless, classic look, placing her in the same company as the "greats" she is paying tribute to on the album. The cover image says that Jenni is not just a banda singer; she is an artist with international potential, and can sing whatever she wants.

The first single released off the album was "A escondidas," made a hit years earlier by Marisela. Jenni's version was her third single to appear on *Billboard*'s Regional Mexican Airplay list, debuting at number 40 on June 6, 2003, and climbing to number 23 on July 17, staying on the list for eight weeks. Jenni was also very pleased to include "Homenaje a mi madre" on the album, a song she wrote for her own mother, Rosa Rivera.

Showing just how far she had come, Jenni celebrated the album's launch with a concert that summer at the historic Ford Amphitheatre in Hollywood, becoming the first regional Mexican artist to perform on that stage.

But bitter disappointments came along hand-in-hand with her triumphs. On April 19, 2003, *Homenaje a las grandes* became Jenni Rivera's first album to debut on *Billboard*'s Top Latin Albums list, which tracks sales of Latin albums all over the country. The record debuted at 70, and rose to number 37, positions which weren't necessarily high, but it was an enormous achievement for an artist who's fame had mostly been concentrated in California and the West Coast. Everything seemed to be coming up roses for Jenni. Except her marriage.

That same April, as her album was released, Jenni separated from Juan Lopez, her second husband.

"I fought, I suffered, but Juan wasn't with me anymore," Jenni explained in an interview with *TVNotas*. "My name was getting bigger, and my husband didn't handle what was happening in our lives very well. There was a lot of fighting and I felt like he wasn't being supportive, and he didn't have faith in what I had done."

Rivera made the decision to separate. She had done all she thought possible to try and save her marriage. And, as she told *La Opinion*, she had consulted a marriage counselor. But things had not gotten better.

"I had to be a little more selfish; and stop thinking about everyone else and think about me," Rivera said. "We had been fighting for a long time. One day I filled out the paperwork, I went down to the courthouse and filed for divorce. He [Juan] never believed that I would do it, but I knew I would have no regrets, that I was doing it for my own happiness. All I wanted was to try to find some peace and calm."

Peace and calm would not come so easily. By late August, when Jenni gave the interview with *La Opinion*, Juan was demanding that Jenni give him a financial settlement after the divorce, and monthly alimony payments to cover all his expenses.

"I'm used to struggling to get ahead, and not take anything from anybody," Jenni said. "I know it's the law and I respect it, but it doesn't seem right to me that [Juan] is asking me to financially support him."

In a September 2003 interview in *Furia Musical*, Jenni was asked if she thought it was fair of Juan to ask for half of everything after their divorce. She replied: "Well, I've always worked hard for my children, they are the most important thing to me, and it's painful for me to see something that belongs to them get taken away. It's not about him or about it, it's about my children and their future, keeping in mind that the two smallest ones are both of ours. But, no doubt, he thinks he has a right to part of whatever was earned while we were together, which I will leave in the hands of the justice system and God."

In the United States, it is customary for the spouse who earns the most to pay support to the other after a divorce, so it is possible that Jenni was legally required to pay spousal support to Juan, whether she agreed with it or not. But it was very clear that she would do all she could to fight for her children.

Jenni never publicly revealed how much she paid in alimony, if any, to Juan, or for how long, and the whole process of the divorce was not easy. "Of course it hurts," she said soon after they separated, in the interview with *Furia Musical*. "Since I'm so busy with work, sometimes I get distracted for a minute and forget about it, but it's very hard to set aside something that was the most important phase in my life. He was a man I loved very much. It's impossible to just wipe out eight years of a shared life from one day to the next. But I'm strong and I'll keep going, I have faith that I can close this chapter."

Jenni did manage to maintain a cordial, positive relationship with her ex-husband after their divorce. Even in the interviews she granted soon after they separated, Jenni never spoke badly of Juan. This was always her approach, throughout her life. When she broke up with Esteban Loaiza years later, she never spoke ill of him in public, either. Jenni was always very respectful of her partners, and always conducted herself with nothing but class when it came to making statements about her personal life in the media. As she said many times, she was always a good wife, and she believed that a husband and wife were a team, who mutually supported each other. She would never be disloyal in that way. She told it like it was in her songs, but she never got into the unseemly habit of saying bad things about the men she had once loved (with the exception of Trino, for obvious reasons). As for Juan, he was not only Jenicka and Johnny's father, he had also acted like a father with Jenni's older three children, who he had known ever since they were small.

But things would end very badly for Juan. Four years later, in October 2007, he was sentenced to three years in prison for drug trafficking. By that time, Jenni was a huge star, having earned countless awards, and having reached the number one spot on *Billboard*'s radio charts and sales charts.

Juan was incarcerated at the California City Correctional Center in Los Angeles, California. Jenni set aside whatever differences she may have had in the past with her ex-husband. They had promised to be friends until the end for their children's sake, and Jenni took them to visit their father as often as she could.

Life behind bars is not easy for those on the inside, or for their family members on the outside. In Jenni's case, all of her children behaved like a cohesive unit, all supporting another. A three-year sentence doesn't exactly pass in the blink of any eye, but it is bearable; Juan Lopez must have been looking forward to seeing Jenicka and Johnny, still children, when he was released. But once again, destiny had other plans.

In June 2009, with over half of his sentence served, Juan Lopez got sick in prison. According to an article published by Bandamax TV, Juan's cellmate said that at first, the prison doctor did not want to attend to him. And when he finally did, Juan was already seriously ill. Then he was rushed to the Antelope Valley Hospital in Lancaster, California on June 17.

His family did not find out about what had happened to Juan until June 23, when he was in critical condition. Jenni and her children went to see him immediately and were constantly at his bedside, until the hospital barred them from visiting, saying they were attracting too much media attention. Not only were Jenni and her children not allowed to visit, Juan's parents were no longer allowed, either. What happened next was one of the most painful episodes in Jenni Rivera's life.

Since Jenni wasn't allowed to visit Juan anymore, she took her children along with her to attend a dedication ceremony for a new music wing at a local school. Meanwhile, in that lonely hospital room, Juan Lopez died . . . all alone.

"My children were at an elementary school with me that was dedicating its new music and arts department, named after me," Jenni said in interviews later. "It was very beautiful. Six hours later, their papi died, all alone, in a hospital in Lancaster."

Juan Lopez died without his family around him. The cause of death was reportedly pulmonary failure, although some sources say it was a heart attack.

"The point is he died alone," Jenni said. "How sad. Because he had been married to and had children with a celebrity." She added that "it's crazy that on the one hand, because of my name and what I've achieved in my career, I'm commemorated and honored, but at the same time they deprive me of the chance to visit the man I once loved in the final moments of his life."

At the end, Jenni offered some words that now seem to sadly foreshadow the future: "[My children] are devastated. They can't believe it. I pray to God to give me the strength and wisdom to guide them in the days to come. The funeral, the burial and the rest of their lives. There's no instruction book on how to be their guide. Their mommy fixes everything, but this can't be fixed."

CHAPTER 12

Becoming the Boss

At some point in her career, Jenni Rivera realized it didn't matter what she did, what she said, who she was with, or what she was wearing, the media was interested in everything. This must have been very satisfying at first. Jenni's career was growing, and every day there was more interest in her music. But then, interest in her music spilled over into interest in her entire life. Jenni wasn't just a woman who sang corridos, or a single mother. She was also Lupillo's sister. And she was the daughter of Pedro Rivera—the man who had released Chalino Sanchez' records on his label. And Chalino Sanchez had sung narcocorridos and had been killed, which gave rise to all kinds of rumors about the Riveras' possible connections to the narco underworld. It didn't matter how many times Jenni denied every rumor and accusation thrown in front of her, there was always something else. The endless questions that arose were often just a reflection of her personal life. Did Jenni just get married, or divorced, had her husband been locked up in jail. The more public appearances Jenni made, the more rumors and interest swirled around her: did Jenni drink on stage, had she gotten drunk, did she take her shoes off, did she tell off some men, had she taken her bra off.

"I say what I think, I am how I am," she told me in the 2010 interview on *Estudio Billboard*. "There are a lot of artists who are artists and in front of the cameras they can say one thing while they really think something else, but the point is to look good. I'm not like that. I am a woman and singing is my job. [...] I get up on stage and I'm the singer, and I get off stage and I'm the woman. That means that because of the things I've said, because of how I'm so frank and direct, it gets the media's attention, they publish it, it goes on the air and that gets the public's attention. When you get the public's attention you're ratings. Whatever you say, whatever you do, your name is ratings. [...] As the human being I am it can be exhausting, but I don't complain. It's part of what I decided to be, and I have to put up with it."

More than anything else, perhaps the most important thing Jenni Rivera had was intelligence. And at some point, it occurred to her she could make something out of this rush of interest.

"When I saw how my life was intriguing to people watching television, I thought I'm going to use *my* name, *my* way. My name gets used in a lot of ways by many different people, so the best way to use the Jenni Rivera name is as the businesswoman I am and say, 'I'm going to produce television shows, I'm going to put out a line of clothing, I'll have perfumes, I'm going to have my own radio show,'" she explained at the *Billboard* Latin Music Conference in 2012.

One of the changes Jenni made in her life was to organize her support team. Up until 2003, she had worked hand in hand with

Jenni Rivera y Leila Cobo en la Conferencia Billboard de Música Mexicana en Los Ángeles en 2009, lugar donde Jenni habló con su familia. Leila le regaló a Jenni una copia de su primera novela, *Tell Me Something True.*

....

Jenni Rivera and Leila Cobo at the Billboard Mexican Music Conference in Los Angeles in 2009, where Jenni spoke with her family. Leila gave Jenni a copy of her first novel, *Tell Me Something True*, during the conference.

Fotos por Arnold Turner, cortesía de Billboard. Copyright 2013. PROMETHEUS Global Media.
Photos by Arnold Turner, courtesy of Billboard. Copyright 2013. PROMETHEUS Global Media.

LA DINASTÍA RIVERA. Jenni posa con su padre y hermanos. De la izquierda: Gustavo Rivera, Don Pedro Rivera, Jenni Rivera, Lupillo Rivera, Pedro Rivera, Jr., Leila Cobo y Juan Rivera.

....

THE RIVERA DYNASTY. Jenni poses with her father and brothers. From left to right: Gustavo Rivera, Don Pedro Rivera, Jenni Rivera, Lupillo Rivera, Pedro Rivera, Jr., Leila Cobo, and Juan Rivera.

Jenni radiante en la alfombra roja durante Los Premios Billboard en 2012.

Jenni sparkles on the red carpet at the Billboard Awards in 2012.

Jenni recibe besos de los músicos Chino & Nacho en la alfombra roja.

Jenni gets a double kiss on the red carpet from singers Chino & Nacho.

Jenni posa junto a su portada.

Jenni poses next to her cover photo.

Jenni da una entrevista a
Billboard.com.

Jenni gives Billboard.com
an interview.

Jenni en el marco de la Conferencia Billboard de la Música Latina. De la izquierda: Bill Werde, director editorial de *Billboard*; Jenni Rivera; Tommy Page, director comercial de *Billboard*; y Leila Cobo.

Jenni on the Billboard Latin Music Conference & Awards stage. From left: Bill Werde, Editorial Director of *Billboard*; Jenni Rivera; Tommy Page, Commercial Director of *Billboard*; and Leila Cobo.

Leila entrevistando a Jenni.

Leila interviewing Jenni.

JENNI RIVERA
TOP LATIN ALBUMS

Debut		Peak		Title Imprint & Number / Label	Artist	Chart Weeks
70	04/19/03	37	05/24/03	**HOMENAJE A LAS GRANDES** Fonovisa 350779 / UMLE	JENNI RIVERA	6
41	10/16/04	29	10/23/04	**SIMPLEMENTE... LA MEJOR!** Univision 310343 / Universal Music Latino	JENNI RIVERA	5
20	10/08/05	10	10/15/05	**PARRANDERA, REBELDE Y ATREVIDA** Fonovisa 352165 / Universal Music Latino	JENNI RIVERA	59
42	05/20/06	39	06/17/06	**EN VIVO DESDE HOLLYWOOD** Fonovisa 352339 / Universal Music Latino	JENNI RIVERA	12
19	09/30/06	19	09/30/06	**BESOS Y COPAS DESDE HOLLYWOOD** Fonovisa 352729 / Universal Music Latino	JENNI RIVERA	7
2	04/21/07	2	04/21/07	**MI VIDA LOCA** Fonovisa 353001 / UMLE	JENNI RIVERA	51
55	11/24/07	33	12/08/07	**LA DIVA EN VIVO!** Fonovisa 353214 / UMLE	JENNI RIVERA	7
1	09/27/08	1[1]	09/27/08	**JENNI** Ayana/Fonovisa 353623 / UMLE	JENNI RIVERA	41
35	08/15/09	13	08/29/09	**JENNI: EDICIÓN CD/ DVD SUPER DELUXE** Ayana/Fonovisa 354092 / UMLE	JENNI RIVERA	12
2	12/19/09	2	12/19/09	**LA GRAN SEÑORA** Fonovisa 354398 / UMLE	JENNI RIVERA	78
8	12/11/10	8	12/11/10	**LA GRAN SEÑORA: EN VIVO** Fonovisa 354603 / UMLE	JENNI RIVERA	28
4	12/10/11	2	12/22/12	**JOYAS PRESTADAS: POP** Fonovisa 354660 / UMLE	JENNI RIVERA	48
2	12/10/11	2	12/10/11	**JOYAS PRESTADAS: BANDA** Fonovisa 354659 / UMLE	JENNI RIVERA	62
1	12/29/12	1[7]	12/29/12	**LA MISMA GRAN SEÑORA** Fonovisa 017911 / UMLE	JENNI RIVERA	7

JENNI RIVERA
HOT LATIN SONGS

Debut		Peak		Title Imprint & Number / Label	Artist	Chart Weeks
37	11/12/05	31	01/14/06	**QUÉ ME VAS A DAR** Fonovisa	JENNI RIVERA	12
40	02/18/06	14	06/03/06	**DE CONTRABANDO** Fonovisa	JENNI RIVERA	20
50	07/15/06	49	07/22/06	**NO VAS A CREER** Fonovisa	JENNI RIVERA	2
46	10/21/06	46	10/21/06	**BESOS Y COPAS** Fonovisa	JENNI RIVERA	1
50	06/16/07	19	08/25/07	**MÍRAME** Fonovisa	JENNI RIVERA	20
45	11/10/07	9	01/26/08	**AHORA QUE ESTUVISTE LEJOS** Fonovisa	JENNI RIVERA	18
43	03/22/08	13	06/14/08	**INOLVIDABLE** Fonovisa	JENNI RIVERA	20
50	03/29/08	48	04/19/08	**COSAS DEL AMOR** Universal Music Latino	OLGA TANON FEATURING MILLY QUEZADA OR JENNI RIVERA	3
30	08/30/08	15	12/06/08	**CULPABLE O INOCENTE** Fonovisa	JENNI RIVERA	21
37	02/21/09	37	02/21/09	**CHUPER AMIGOS** Fonovisa	JENNI RIVERA	7
43	06/06/09	24	07/25/09	**TU CAMISA PUESTA** Fonovisa	JENNI RIVERA	13
22	08/15/09	22	08/15/09	**OVARIOS** Fonovisa	JENNI RIVERA	10
33	12/19/09	16	02/27/10	**YA LO SÉ** Fonovisa	JENNI RIVERA	20
49	07/17/10	46	08/21/10	**POR QUÉ NO LE CALAS** Fonovisa	JENNI RIVERA	3
47	04/09/11	44	04/30/11	**LA GRAN SEÑORA** Fonovisa	JENNI RIVERA	7
40	09/17/11	14	12/10/11	**BASTA YA** Fonovisa / UMLE	JENNI RIVERA FEATURING MARCO ANTONIO SOLIS	21
49	06/09/12	49	06/09/12	**A CAMBIO DE QUÉ** Fonovisa / UMLE	JENNI RIVERA	1
32	09/22/12	12	12/29/12	**DETRÁS DE MI VENTANA** Fonovisa / UMLE	JENNI RIVERA	20
43	11/17/12	9	01/05/13	**LA MISMA GRAN SEÑORA** Fonovisa / UMLE	JENNI RIVERA	12
28	12/29/12	28	12/29/12	**COMO TU MUJER** Fonovisa / UMLE	JENNI RIVERA FEATURING MARCO ANTONIO SOLIS	3
37	12/29/12	37	12/29/12	**A QUE NO LE CUENTAS** Fonovisa / UMLE	JENNI RIVERA	2
33	12/29/12	33	12/29/12	**ASÍ FUE** Fonovisa / UMLE	JENNI RIVERA	2

JENNI RIVERA
REGIONAL MEXICAN ALBUMS

Debut		Peak		Title Imprint & Number / Label	Artist	Chart Weeks
20	10/23/04	**20**	10/23/04	**SIMPLEMENTE… LA MEJOR!** Univision 310343 / Universal Music Latino	JENNI RIVERA	1
9	10/08/05	**2**	10/15/05	**PARRANDERA, REBELDE Y ATREVIDA** Fonovisa 352165 / Universal Music Latino	JENNI RIVERA	32
16	05/20/06	**13**	06/17/06	**EN VIVO DESDE HOLLYWOOD** Fonovisa / Universal Music Latino	JENNI RIVERA	6
6	09/30/06	**5**	10/07/06	**BESOS Y COPAS DESDE HOLLYWOOD** Fonovisa / Universal Music Latino	JENNI RIVERA	6
1	04/21/07	**1**¹	04/21/07	**MI VIDA LOCA** Fonovisa / UMLE	JENNI RIVERA	16
11	12/08/07	**11**	12/08/07	**LA DIVA EN VIVO!** Fonovisa 353214 / UMLE	JENNI RIVERA	3
1	09/27/08	**1**¹	09/27/08	**JENNI** Ayana/Fonovisa 353623 / UMLE	JENNI RIVERA	28
18	08/22/09	**9**	08/29/09	**JENNI: EDICIÓN CD/ DVD SUPER DELUXE** Ayana/Fonovisa 354092 / UMLE	JENNI RIVERA	4
1	12/19/09	**1**⁴	12/19/09	**LA GRAN SEÑORA** Fonovisa 354398 / UMLE	JENNI RIVERA	61
2	12/11/10	**2**	12/11/10	**LA GRAN SEÑORA: EN VIVO** Fonovisa 354603 / UMLE	JENNI RIVERA	19
1	12/10/11	**1**⁵	12/10/11	**JOYAS PRESTADAS: BANDA** Fonovisa 354659 / UMLE	JENNI RIVERA	47
1	12/29/12	**1**⁷	12/29/12	**LA MISMA GRAN SEÑORA** Fonovisa 017911 / UMLE	JENNI RIVERA	7

JENNI RIVERA
REGIONAL MEXICAN AIRPLAY

	Debut		Peak	Title Imprint & Number / Label	Artist	Chart Weeks
25	04/21/01	18	04/28/01	**QUERIDA SOCIA** Fonovisa	JENNI RIVERA	17
31	04/06/02	16	04/13/02	**ANGEL BABY** Discos Cisne	JENNI RIVERA	7
40	06/28/03	23	07/19/03	**A ESCONDIDAS** Fonovisa	JENNI RIVERA	8
37	02/21/04	37	02/21/04	**JURO QUE NUNCA VOLVERÉ** Fonovisa	JENNI RIVERA	1
35	03/12/05	35	03/12/05	**AMIGA, SI LO VES** Univision	JENNI RIVERA	4
29	09/03/05	7	12/17/05	**QUÉ ME VAS A DAR** Fonovisa	JENNI RIVERA	23
30	01/28/06	1¹	06/03/06	**DE CONTRABANDO** Fonovisa	JENNI RIVERA	33
35	06/24/06	13	07/15/06	**NO VAS A CREER** Fonovisa	JENNI RIVERA	11
39	08/26/06	10	10/21/06	**BESOS Y COPAS** Fonovisa	JENNI RIVERA	23
37	03/10/07	23	04/14/07	**LA SOPA DEL BEBÉ** Fonovisa	JENNI RIVERA	8
28	05/12/07	8	08/25/07	**MÍRAME** Fonovisa	JENNI RIVERA	27
28	10/20/07	3	01/26/08	**AHORA QUE ESTUVISTE LEJOS** Fonovisa	JENNI RIVERA	21
36	03/08/08	5	06/14/08	**INOLVIDABLE** Fonovisa	JENNI RIVERA	25
30	08/16/08	4	12/06/08	**CULPABLE O INOCENTE** Fonovisa	JENNI RIVERA	26
30	02/07/09	19	02/21/09	**CHUPER AMIGOS** Fonovisa	JENNI RIVERA	10
32	05/23/09	13	07/18/09	**TU CAMISA PUESTA** Fonovisa	JENNI RIVERA	19
29	08/08/09	13	08/15/09	**OVARIOS** Fonovisa	JENNI RIVERA	12
39	11/28/09	7	02/27/10	**YA LO SÉ** Fonovisa	JENNI RIVERA	28
36	05/15/10	22	08/14/10	**POR QUÉ NO LE CALAS** Fonovisa	JENNI RIVERA	20
37	11/06/10	31	12/18/10	**DÉJAME VOLVER CONTIGO** Fonovisa	JENNI RIVERA	12
37	01/01/11	25	01/07/12	**AMARGA NAVIDAD** Fonovisa / UMLE	JENNI RIVERA	4
39	02/19/11	23	05/07/11	**LA GRAN SEÑORA** Fonovisa	JENNI RIVERA	20
30	09/10/11	6	12/10/11	**BASTA YA** Fonovisa / UMLE	JENNI RIVERA FEATURING MARCO ANTONIO SOLIS	28
35	03/31/12	21	07/14/12	**A CAMBIO DE QUÉ** Fonovisa / UMLE	JENNI RIVERA	19
39	08/04/12	6	11/03/12	**DETRÁS DE MI VENTANA** Fonovisa / UMLE	JENNI RIVERA	20
16	11/17/12	6	12/29/12	**LA MISMA GRAN SEÑORA** Fonovisa / UMLE	JENNI RIVERA	13

her husband Juan, who had helped her with all aspects of her career and day-to-day tasks. And she had a team that included the well-known music lawyer Anthony Lopez, who was also her brother Lupillo's lawyer. When Jenni and Juan separated, Lopez called up Pete Gonzalez, who at the time was working as the business manager for the group Los Tucanes de Tijuana, and Juan suggested he get in touch with Jenni.

"I met Jenni and she had bigger balls than most of the men I've worked with," Gonzalez remarked in an interview for *Billboard* magazine in December 2012. "We connected. I knew I wanted to be a part of what she was going to do."

With Gonzalez now at her side, Jenni's team was in place. It's important to remember that Jenni handled her career in a very businesslike way, ever since the beginning. She understood she needed someone to manage the business aspects, and someone to handle publicity. She had a makeup artist, a hair stylist, and a designer. Jenni understood the importance of investing in her career, and how important it was that she control her own image and her product.

"I still think of myself more as a businesswoman than an artist," she told me during the *Billboard* Conference in 2012. "Even when I'm on stage, I know I'm getting paid, but that's like a kind of therapy. It's a release of everything I'm living. The work is traveling, promoting, but being on stage—those three hours I sing—is really the fun part of all this."

By 2003, Jenni was very established as a singer who was constantly performing. In this regard she was not unique. In the world of regional Mexican music, groups and solo artists of the genre are always touring. They play almost every single weekend in all kinds of venues, from arenas and discos to outdoor fairs and clubs. Jenni did all of that, but at the same time she was a diva, and performed on grand stages like the Staples Center, the Nokia Theater, Mexico's Auditorio Nacional, and the Ford Amphitheatre, where no regional Mexican artist had ever performed before. Jenni knew how to inhabit the world of Mexican music, only with the "diva" attitude of megastars such as Paulina Rubio and Thalia. But she didn't limit herself to that role: Jenni loved performing live, and she loved connecting with her fans. Being untouchable was unthinkable to her. Her fans gave her energy and life, and she recognized that.

"The love you get from the fans is very special," she said in an interview on Radio al Aire while promoting *Homenaje a las grandes* in 2003. "It's something unique that my parents, my brothers and sister, my children, or my partner can't give me. It's a very different kind of love that many artists don't appreciate, and it goes unnoticed. The fans are really important to me, and I like to give them the love and attention they deserve."

Jenni always listened to her fans, and the more her fan base grew, the bigger she got. In 2004, in an effort to grow her audience and expand her own horizons, Jenni took an interesting step: she signed with the label Univision Records.

Univision Records had been formed in 2001 as part of Univision Communications, but it operated as an independent entity. Univision was a label with a wide range of artists in its catalog, but between 2001 and 2002, the company bought Fonovisa, the biggest label for regional Mexican music in the world, and the label that Jenni worked with the most.

Jenni was very happy at Fonovisa—in fact, Fonovisa and Univision shared the same administration and president—but Univision was seen as a more international, major label, which could work with Jenni not only in the Mexican music orbit but also in the world of pop. So on November 4, 2004, Jenni released *Simplemente . . . La Mejor*, a CD/DVD set featuring her greatest hits, including corridos like "Las Malandrinas" and "La Chacalosa," and others like "Querida socia" and "Se las voy a dar a otro." The album also included several rough cuts, such as "Amiga si lo ves" by Yaredt Leon, the first pop version of a song Jenni ever recorded. Although the song wasn't a big hit on the radio—it was on the Regional Mexican Airplay chart for four weeks, peaking at just 35—it did signal a turning point in Jenni's career, showing that she could cross over into different genres, and it revealed her vulnerable side. In "Amiga si lo ves," she's not the fighter who comes out of a bad relationship stronger than ever; she's a woman who has lost the man she loves, and she still longs for him. "This song is very special to me, because I've always sung about things that I can feel, or I feel have happened to other people," Jenni said in the press release announcing the song's release. "A song like 'Amiga si lo ves' describes a woman's feelings, no matter how strong she may be, or whoever she may be, we've all suffered for love."

The video of "Amiga si lo ves" also marks a new level of artistic expression for Jenni. Directed by Risa Machuca and produced by the acclaimed Dominican film and music video director Jessy Terrero, it is a small film in itself, dedicated to everyone who has ever lost a loved one. Instead of simply featuring a woman in emotional pain, the video tells several interconnected stories of people who have lost the ones they love the most in their lives, from children to parents. It may be the most beautiful video in Jenni's entire catalog.

"In the pop version, the emotion comes across stronger, and for me it's important to be versatile and show it's not just *corridos* and *ranchera* songs, with strong themes, I want to show that just like every woman, I have my moments of sadness," Jenni explained in an interview with New York's *El Diario la Prensa* on December 2.

While Jenni ventured out of her musical comfort zone singing pop, she also began exploring new territory on the business side. Between 2003 and 2005, Jenni began serious plans to launch a fragrance and a makeup line. The brand would be called Divina, as Jenni explained, because she wanted all women to feel divine, inside and out.

In an interview published in *Vida en el Valle* in February 2005, Jenni said she had worked on developing her cosmetics line for two years, conducting research and having meetings with manufactures of cosmetics ingredients.

"Very high-quality cosmetics are expensive, and my fans can't afford high-quality cosmetics," she said in the interview, explaining why she had decided to launch her new product line.

Several months later, in November of that year, her sister Rosie posted in a forum on Univision.com, announcing the launch of the line, which included lipsticks with the colorful names Rosa Rosita, Chiquis, and Juicy Jackie. Profits from the sale of those shades would be donated to Jenni's foundation.

And Jenni still had her real estate office, her first profession which had allowed her to be self-sufficient and not have to depend on public assistance.

"She understood her identity as a brand," her manager Pete Salgado said in an interview with *Billboard* following Jenni's death. "She understood she was Coca-Cola. And things started to be done on her terms in every aspect. She was the best marketing expert I've ever known. She was focused. And it was hard to keep up with her pace. She's a person who gets up at six in the morning, ready to get to work."

Jenni had just begun to build her empire, but she already knew what course it would take.

CHAPTER

13

Singing to Life . . . and to Death

J enni always loved to sing what she lived, or what her fans lived. Her songs were often stories, describing things that happened in real life. If it hadn't happened to her, it had happened to somebody else. And if Jenni didn't really feel the truth in the lyrics, she wouldn't sing it. That was a part of her incredibly strong connection with her fans. She thought — correctly — that a large part of her success was due to her honesty, her integrity as a person both on- and offstage, and the fact that she never forgot the person she had once been, and she never lost touch with the people who made her who she was: her fans.

"For those of us who make our livings singing, we must never forget where we came from," Jenni said in an interview with *Radio Notas* in 2002. "Humility is something we should always have through our whole life. [. . .] Being Jenni Rivera the recording artist doesn't mean I'm better than anyone else, it's just that God gave me this gift, this opportunity to record, and for people to listen to me. There are a lot of people who think they're a big deal, they treat their fans badly and they don't understand that the fans are how we make a living, the fans bought my car, the fans put gas in my car, the fans put clothes on my back, the fans feed me, and there are a lot of artists who just don't see that."

Jenni didn't write all of her songs, usually just one or two of the songs on any one album were her compositions. The rest came from songwriters, big and small, who were able to channel Jenni's experiences into words and music that reflected the singer's most heartfelt emotions. All of Jenni's albums are personal, and all tell stories that deeply touched her. But two in particular are very closely associated with la Diva de la Banda's life: *Parrandera, rebelde y atrevida* (2005) and *Mi vida loca* (2007).

Off of *Parrandera, rebelde y atrevida* the single "De contrabando" was released, written by Joan Sebastian, a great friend of Jenni's. In June 2006, the song claimed the number one spot on the Regional Mexican Airplay chart in *Billboard*, becoming Jenni's first and only number one song. It stayed at number one for a week, and was on the chart for a total of thirty-three weeks. The album *Parrandera, rebelde y atrevida* debuted at number two on the Regional Mexican Albums chart, and at number ten on the list of Top Latin Albums. It was the highest-ranking debut for an album Jenni had ever had, and it stayed on the charts for fifty-nine weeks—over a year.

"I liked 'De contrabando' a lot because it talks about the other woman, she knows she shouldn't be with that man, but she likes it," Jenni told me on *Estudio Billboard*. "And that's contraband love [amor de contrabando]."

But that wasn't the only song that sold the album. The title track, *Parrandera, rebelde y atrevida*, was like an irresistible invitation to listen. The lyrics of the song evoked another of Jenni's big hits, "Las Malandrinas," saying I'm a party girl, rebellious and in your face, I'm a *ranchera* girl, that's in my heart, bitter champagne is for stuck-up old ladies, I want my Tecate with salt and lemon.

Incredibly, all these years after "Las Malandrinas," and even after a hit song with a similar theme was released in the general market—Gretchen Wilson's "Redneck Woman"—Jenni was still the only Latina artist who sang honestly and frankly, telling it like it is, talking about what it was like to be a regular girl from the barrio. This wasn't a song sung by a diva or a pop star. It was just the story of a woman who liked to go out and party. The fans loved it.

"Some people think it's wrong, but singing that you like to go out with your girlfriends and have a few drinks are things that everyone does, but we're afraid to sing about it," Jenni told me on *Estudio Billboard* in 2010. "And I said, no. I know what I'm doing. I know what my fans are like, my girls. They like to hear songs about real life. And when I'm recording it I go, 'we're going to see what happens.' But when the record started to sell, and when they were requesting the song on the radio, and when I'm on stage and they ask for the songs I wrote, I think 'no, that wasn't bad at all.'"

In spite of the partying spirit around it, and in spite of its major success, *Parrandera, rebelde y atrevida* also held a dark note of premonition, captured in the song "Cuando muere una dama" [when a lady dies]. Jenni had tackled the subject of death at various times over the course of career. Years earlier, she had recorded "Que me entierren con la banda" with her brother

Lupillo, but that song, in which the singer asks to be buried with the band, was written by Melo Diaz and popularized long before Jenni sang it. In contrast, "Cuando muere una dama" was written by Jenni herself, after she had a very close call with death.

On May 16, 2005, Jenni suffered a car accident which did not result in any serious injuries, but which could have been deadly. Jenni was driving near her home in Corona when she fell asleep behind the wheel and was hit by another car. Luckily, it was a side impact, not a head-on collision; otherwise, Jenni could have died.

"The loss of the car isn't so important, that's just material," her sister Rosie Rivera said at the time on an interview on Bang Bang radio. "But to think that my sister could have died, that terrifies me. I'm so thankful to our Lord, because it's a real miracle."

The incident gave Jenni such a scare that she spoke publicly about how the accident had prompted her to reflect on life and the possibility of death.

"The accident made me think about how I'd like to be sent off (when I have to go), if that had really happened," she said, also on Bang Bang Radio. "The inspiration came to me spontaneously, and it's been a big help because it's a way for me to express my feelings and the fear I felt afterwards. I'm very grateful to God, for allowing me to continue on in this world, with my loved ones around me. Maybe my mother's prayers reached me, and now I can appreciate the opportunity that life is giving me."

Listening to "Cuando muere una dama" now, after Jenni has actually died, is as sad as it is revealing. In the song, Jenni clearly explains how she would like to be celebrated, and remembered. Many things she expresses in the lyrics—the peace of arriving at "another show" up in heaven, how she would look and how she wanted to be remembered, even including instructions for her funeral service (specifying she wanted butterflies released, and asking her sister to "read my letter"), underscores just how closely Jenni was tied to her songs, since she sang this in 2005 and it's basically what was done in 2012 after her death.

"Cuando muere una dama" was the last song on *Parrandera, rebelde y atrevida* and was never a single that got much radio play. But just as with all of Jenni's songs, her fans knew it very well and asked for it at shows. Looking back to 2005 and 2006, Jenni Rivera was at her zenith, and was definitely the most famous woman performing in regional Mexican music. Her album climbed to the number one position on the *Billboard* Top Regional Mexican Albums chart—a feat only made possible by many thousands and thousands of fans buying the record.

Jenni not only performed every weekend—Fridays, Saturdays, and Sundays, and sometimes even on Thursdays—and worked at a frenetic pace during the week, she was also starting to fill venues usually reserved for major pop stars. In 2006, for example, she sold out the prestigious Gibson Amphitheatre in Los Angeles (where her memorial service would be held after her death), making her the first regional Mexican artist to accomplish this.

It seemed that around 2006 and 2007, Jenni's fame had reached its peak. But it hadn't. Not yet. As a celebrity, she was just starting to spread her wings. What this warrior butterfly managed to achieve in the last five years of her life was nothing short of extraordinary.

CHAPTER
14

My Crazy Life

O n October 15, 2005, Jenni had performed a sold-out show at the Kodak Theater. Then on August 5, 2006, she made history: she gave a concert at the larger Gibson Amphitheatre in Los Angeles, which holds over 6,000 seats, and that show was also a total sellout. For Jenni, this was a major accomplishment. She had performed for years on all kinds of stages, in nightclubs, street fairs and concert halls, but selling out the Gibson meant she was at the same lofty level as any major pop star. At the end of the show, her label, Fonovisa presented her with a Platinum record, commemorating over 200,000 in sales in the United States for her record *Parrandera, rebelde y atrevida*. Jenni wore one of her mermaid-style dresses, bright fuchsia, hugging her curves, spreading out below her knees. She looked stunning and radiant.

That same year, affirming that as a live performer she had no equal, Jenni released two live albums. The first CD/DVD set, *En vivo desde Hollywood* went on sale on May 2, 2006, followed by *Besos y copas, en vivo desde Hollywood*, released on September

12, 2006. Both albums climbed the *Billboard* charts, released barely four months apart. *En vivo desde Hollywood* debuted at number 16 on the Regional Mexican Albums chart, peaking at number 13, staying on the chart for six weeks. It peaked at 39 on the Top Latin Albums chart, staying on that list for twelve weeks. *Besos y copas, en vivo desde Hollywood*, released after the historic concert at the Gibson, debuted at number 6 on the Regional Mexican Albums chart, rising to number 5, and also stayed on the list for six weeks. On September 30, that album debuted at 19 on the Top Latin Albums chart, staying on the list for seven weeks.

All of these remarkable achievements could be seen as a prelude to what would be Jenni Rivera's master work: *Mi vida loca* [my crazy life]. The album, released on April 21, 2007, (coinciding with the *Billboard Latin Music Awards*), debuted at number 2 on the Top Latin Albums chart, and at number 1 on the Top Regional Mexican Albums chart. It was the first of Jenni's albums to reach number 1, but it wouldn't be the last.

Aside from the stellar sales, *Mi vida loca* was a kind of musical autobiography (in fact, Jenni always said the memoir she was writing would be titled *Mi vida loca*), at times brutally honest, and with a spoken-word introduction at the top of every song.

"Music was what helped me get ahead, it gave me the strength to get up after every fall, every stumble," Jenni told me on *Estudio Billboard*. "And on my record *Mi vida loca*, I'm singing it. It's called *Mi vida loca* because I'm singing about different really difficult experiences I've lived through, and before every song I talk about why I'm singing about it, and a little about the experience I went through."

Jenni explained that it had taken her some time to get to the point where she could make a record as deeply personal as *Mi vida loca*. She had always sung about her experiences and feelings before, but never in such an open way, and she had never tried to tell her whole life story in an album.

"I think I had the idea in my head for about three years," Jenni said in an interview with *Billboard* in 2007 when the album was released. "I wanted to wait for the right moment. I think some things had to happen first, not only in my personal life, but in my career. I had to grow, and during that process, I realized that people were genuinely interested and intrigued by what happened in my life. They feel like I am like them. I'm a normal person, but I sing and work. So they identify with me, but they want to know more about me."

Some of the songs on *Mi vida loca* made references to very specific, personal things: "Sangre de Indio," [Indian blood] dedicated to Pedro Rivera, and sung as a duet with her brother Lupillo; "Cuanto te debo," [How much do I owe you], alluding to the spousal support that Jenni had pay after her divorce, which had so offended her; "Hermano amigo," dedicated to her siblings; and the single "La sopa del bebé," [baby soup], a fun and scandalous song, tells the story of a woman getting back at her cheating husband, luring him into her bedroom, and then telling him "if the mattress is stained/it's baby soup."

The song, as Jenni told *Billboard* when it was released, "is about an unfaithful husband and you give it right back to him, giving him a taste of his own medicine."

An especially important song for Jenni on the album was "Mírame" [Look at me]. Written by Bruno Danza, it's the story of a woman who finds happiness again after the end of a rocky relationship, then she runs into the man who had treated her so badly, but now she's the one doing fine, and he's struggling: "Look at me, it's a pleasure to run into you/now that you're so sad, and I'm so happy," she sang on the chorus.

Although Jenni had not written the song, she sang it with someone very specific in mind: her first husband, Trino. The man she had had her first child with at only fifteen, who had abused her, the man who had sexually abused her daughter and her younger sister.

Talking about what had happened publicly, which seemed too "risky" to the record label, turned out to be something the fans really appreciated and valued, Jenni explained on the television news magazine show *Aquí y Ahora* in February 2011. "They were the ones telling me where I could find him. And they told me, they couldn't stand that he had hit me. My brothers taught me how to box, and I could give two or three good kidney punches. But he thought he could. By then I was Jenni Rivera. He thought, 'you were my wife, I put you in your place,' and thanks to my fans they found him, and arrested him."

And that's how it happened. The world knew what Trino had done, and at one point Lupillo offered a generous cash reward for information leading to his arrest. And Jenni's fans told them where he was. So on April 22, 2006, Trino was arrested in Riverside, Florida, and sent to Long Beach to stand trial.

Trino's trial was extremely emotional. Jenni, Chiquis and Rosie all testified, and the painful process had a profound impact on the whole family. It was incredibly hard for his children, who had not seen him in nine years, to be reunited with their father under such horrible circumstances.

A year later, in June 2007, Trinidad "Trino" Marin, forty-three years old, was sentenced to thirty-one years in prison.

"You're never satisfied," Jenni said on *Aquí y Ahora*. "It's not a pretty story. The only satisfaction I have is that he can't hurt any other little girls any more."

Trino not only abused Jenni and their daughters physically, he also hurt them emotionally. He insulted and degraded Jenni constantly, trying to prop up his own self-esteem, as Jenni described to me on *Estudio Billboard* in 2010: "When we separated and I started singing, he was always telling me that I wouldn't do it, that I'd never amount to anything. And when he began to realize that Jenni was spreading her wings, [. . .] he couldn't stand that I was a butterfly in flight, and not the caterpillar he was used to stepping on."

All of these feelings pour out of *Mi vida loca*. The introduction to "Mírame" is basically Jenni speaking directly to Trino: "I'll never forget what you said: stop singing, you're never going to be somebody . . . Now I'm fighting the most important court case in my life with that man . . ."

"Mírame," Jenni told me, "is talking exactly about that person who told me I'd never amount to anything, who I suffered so much with, and now he's behind bars for thirty-one years, seeing me on a television screen, and hearing me on the radio all the time. I really like that song. I think we can all relate to it, and not just women; at my shows a lot of men sing along. Because men have suffered with women who don't appreciate them. And it makes me really happy that they get it too."

The last song on *Mi vida loca* is "Mariposa de barrio," a song that so proudly describes what Jenni Rivera was, and will always be: "Butterfly from the barrio, who goes through life singing, the caterpillar has transformed its pain into color!" The song, written by Jenni herself, is a metaphor for her life. It's a song of hope for everyone who believes it's possible to change, it's possible to rise up.

"I've gone through so much, but I'm not a victim," Jenni said many times in her life. "I'm not a victim. If I felt like a victim, I couldn't be successful and be where I am now. I have the heart of a warrior."

Jenni, who always shared her records with her father, remembered what he said about *Mi vida loca* in a 2009 interview with *Billboard* magazine: "He said, 'daughter this record is really, really beautiful.' He was always worried that I wouldn't be able to improve on the success of the previous record. And he said, 'I don't know how you're going to top this one, because it's great.'"

In the end, the great triumph of *Mi vida loca* was that it told a serious, harrowing true story, and mesmerized listeners with the warrior spirit her fans loved so much.

CHAPTER 15

The Divine, Protective Lady

One of Jenni's greatest talents was her ability to take some thing negative and turn it into something positive. Jenni did this her whole life; she somehow found a way to vault over every obstacle and turn it into an opportunity. Merriam-Webster's English Dictionary defines "optimism" as "a doctrine that this world is the best possible world." Jenni was most definitely an optimist. It didn't matter how bad the circumstances were, she could turn it around. She seemed to personify the old adage, "when life gives you lemons, make lemonade."

In one especially light-hearted episode, she sold T-shirts with a mug shot of herself on the front, taken when she had been arrested (and quickly released) for having hit a member of the audience with her microphone at a show. But there was nothing funny about the incident that had inspired the T-shirts. It had happened at a June 2008 concert in Raleigh, North Carolina, when in the middle of the performance, someone threw a beer can onto the stage, hitting Jenni. When she asked who had done it, a man raised his hand. He was brought up on stage, where

Jenni unceremoniously hit him in the forehead with her microphone.

The result? Jenni was arrested, escorted from the stage and had to post bail before she could leave the precinct.

"All I can say is that I'm not exactly happy about it, but I do take responsibility for the things I do," she said on an interview with a Los Angeles radio station shortly after the incident. To make matters worse, the fan who she had struck said later that he hadn't even been the one who threw the can. He just raised his hand because he thought he might get to go up on stage and dance with Jenni.

By 2011 Jenni could laugh about it, although it had caused quite a stir at the time, and explained why she decided to sell the T-shirts. "Well the mug shot was already out there, and I thought, if my fans love me so much then they can buy a T-shirt. I try to find something positive in everything," Jenni said in an interview on the television show *Aquí y Ahora*.

J enni had many challenges, dramas and tragedies in her short life. But nothing was so painful as the abuse that she, her sister and her daughters suffered at the hands of her first husband. And she even managed to turn that into something positive, that would have a deep impact on many people.

When Jenni confronted her ex-husband's abuse, she realized that she was not alone. There were many other people like her and her family, and she felt immediately that she had to do something to help them. That was how the Jenni Rivera Love Foundation came to be. Initially founded to aid families who were victims of abuse, today the foundation helps needy families in many areas, providing scholarships, financial aid and educational support, among many other things. And Jenni expanded her charitable giving in several directions, constantly donating to organizations like Children's Hospital, and frequently, spontaneously giving of herself, donating money, objects and time to help others.

There are hundreds of anecdotes about Jenni's generosity: the gown she donated to the Radioton de la Esperanza [Radiothon of Hope] after a show; the money she gave to a child in Mexico so that his family could pay for a kidney transplant; the car she gave to a father in need; the countless sums of money she donated to educational and health centers; the many hours she dedicated to visiting and helping sick children.

As the daughter of undocumented immigrants, Jenni was outspoken in her support of the immigrant cause. When the infamous immigration law SB 1070 was introduced in Arizona in 2010, many artists came out against it. But on May 29, Jenni was the first to go to Arizona and join the crowd of roughly 70,000 marchers who gathered at the capital building in Phoenix to protest the law. Then she gave a concert for the protesters, accompanied by her band, who traveled from Mazatlan, Mexico especially for the show.

"I came here with my children," Jenni said that day. "We left Los Angeles at two o'clock in the morning and drove here in a truck, with my children and my team and we marched. Why? Because it matters to us. It's very important that my granddaughter, who's six months old, will read about this historic moment in a school book someday. I want her to know that her grandmother is always ready to defend her people. I want to raise her to be the same way. And I want our people to see this. I think it's important to remember that these people support us, they go to our shows, they turn on the television to see us. If these people aren't here, who's going to support us?"

The Arizona Law, as it came to be known, awakened a sense of justice in Jenni. As she said then, we weren't in the Second World War, when the Japanese Americans in the United States were singled out. We weren't in Hitler's Germany, when the Jews were singled out, or in the sixties in this country when the African Americans were targeted. "Now it's happening to us," she said. "Someone has to stop them."

By April 2012, when she spoke at the *Billboard Latin Music Conference*, Jenni had refined her views; aside from immigration laws, she thought it was important for Latinos to flex their political muscle. "Political influence is very important," she said at the conference. "When I started singing, I never imagined that I could inspire anybody or have any influence over anything. No I think we can. And we singers who have a big following of fans, I think it's our responsibility not only to share our music but to show that we are united, and that our word, our vote does count. Because it's very easy to just leave it up to the people who we think are in charge of all that. But the census that's coming out is very important and our vote, our yes or no, means a lot. And if I can help with that, I want to tell my people. That we are important, we're very important, even more than we think, not just in politics but on television, in everything. We are many. We are the biggest minority in the country."

But Jenni made her biggest mark as an activist as a tireless crusader against domestic violence and sexual abuse. Aside from the work her foundation did, her impact on the issue was recognized when on August 4, 2010, the National Coalition Against Domestic Violence (NCADV) named her their spokesperson at a conference in Anaheim.

"We are very happy that Jenni Rivera has joined forces with the NCADV to create more awareness, offer hope and inspire others to help us in our mission to make every home a safe home," Rita Smith, the Executive Director of NCDAV said. "Her experience, talent and commitment to end domestic violence are a great gift and we are excited to work with her on many projects."

Being chosen as the spokesperson for the NCDAV was a great honor for Jenni. The NCADV is a prestigious organization that has worked for over thirty-four years to end violence against women, raising awareness and educating the public on the effects of domestic violence. The organization supports more than 50,000 centers and programs all around the world. As part of her new role, Jenni attended several conferences where she spoke about her experiences as a survivor of domestic violence, in an effort to educate other women who may have been going through something similar.

Jenni never stopped talking about it over the years, and in October 2012, when she was named one of the 25 most powerful Latina women by *People en Español* magazine, she nominated her sister as one of the candidates who readers could vote for, to be a part of the list. Rosie Rivera was the director of the Jenni Rivera Love Foundation, and at only thirty-one, she was a preacher for the Unidas Vencermos de la Iglesia Primer Amor of

Long Beach. She often talked about her experience as a survivor of abuse, and she was a captivating speaker.

When the votes from readers were counted, Rosie was the top candidate, so she was also included on the *People en Español* list of 25 most powerful Latina women. On the day of the lunch honoring the 25 named to the list in Miami, among the speakers were Olga Tañón, Lily Estefan, and Jenni, eloquent as ever. As she finished her speech, Jenni introduced her younger sister. As soon as Rosie began speaking, it was immediately apparent to everyone in the room why she had won. I have rarely heard such an emotional, spellbinding talk as Rosie gave at that lunch. She was completely honest about the abuse she had suffered, how it had affected her, and how she had found it in her heart to forgive and help others. If Jenni was an inspiration for many, her little sister was clearly following in her footsteps. It was very obvious that day why Jenni had placed Rosie at the head of the Jenni Rivera Love Foundation to carry on her legacy.

CHAPTER

16

Dreams Come True

By 2008, Jenni Rivera was a superstar in the United States and Mexico. She performed every weekend that year, constantly appeared on television, and the media could not get enough of her.

She had first ascended to that stratosphere of success the year before, when she won the *Billboard* Award for Regional Mexican Song of the Year, Female, for her hit "De contrabando." At the Premios Lo Nuestro, she won Female Artist of the Year in the Regional Mexican category. "I'm very happy. Thankful to God and my fans who have supported my music, and as I always say, I'm representing our musical genre and our Mexican people here at Premio lo Nuestro," she said to Tony Dandrades at the awards ceremony.

Jenni also took the stage that night to present an award to Victor Manuelle, and to sing her award-winning song "De contrabando."

In 2008, the number of awards grew. At the *Billboard* Awards, *Mi vida loca* won the Regional Mexican Album of the Year by a

Female artist, and her song "Mírame" won for Regional Song of the Year by a Female artist. At the Lo Nuestro awards, she once again won Female Artist of the Year. She was also nominated for her second Latin Grammy that year, in the Best Ranchero Album category, for *La Diva en Vivo!*

Her momentum continued to accelerate, and in September 2008, Jenni finally debuted at number one on *Billboard*'s Top Latin Albums chart—the list of the highest selling Latin albums in the country—with her album *Jenni.* Also that year, four of Jenni's singles made the Hot Latin Songs chart, including "Cosas del amor," a song by Olga Tañón which featured Jenni as a guest artist.

Meanwhile, Jenni seriously explored opportunities related to music but in other areas. Over the course of her career, and after having triumphed in the wake of so many truly difficult experiences, it became clear that her sharp business sense allowed her to oversee her career like a corporation. It was also increasingly obvious that Jenni had a gift for more than just singing. When she appeared at awards shows the ratings went through the roof; when she was interviewed on television, whether she was talking about her music or some controversy, viewers were glued to their screens. The charisma Jenni radiated on stage carried over into other areas, and offers started to roll in, seeking to capitalize on her strong bond with her fans. As Jenni herself said, she had always possessed an uncanny ability to forge a connection with people, ever since she was a little girl. But thanks to her music, she could exercise this talent to its maximum potential.

"Everything came from music," she said at the *Billboard* conference in 2012. "Because through my music, I've revealed who

I am. Not just as an artist, but as a woman. I live, express, and interpret my music so they can know that if I didn't actually live the story, someone is living it right now. That's a big part of it. The rest is what I've always been. I was always an entrepreneur. Ever since I sold chewing gum in school and sold my grades and test answers at school. I was always selling something. Even my professor at business school told me, 'You have to sell something, you have to market something.' That always stayed in my head. I never imagined that I would end up selling myself. It all comes from music, but the entrepreneur was there before. The two joined together and made an entertainer."

Jenni was always a tireless worker. But now she put her foot on the accelerator. Everything she had planted the seeds for in 2008 was ready for harvest in 2009, and the results were stunning. The year opened with the announcement that she was a six-time finalist for the *Billboard Latin Music Awards*. Her success was such that she had not one, but two songs nominated for Hot Latin Song of the Year: "Culpable o inocente" and "Inolvidable."

In the midst of all of these impressive achievements, in February 2009, before awards season got underway, Jenni took the money she had worked so hard for and treated herself, purchasing her dream house in Encino, California. It was a mansion with seven bedrooms and eleven bathrooms which her fans would get to see in great detail the following year when Jenni launched her own television reality show, "I Love Jenni," on the network Mun2.

Once the sale was finalized it was announced in the *Los Angeles Times*, which reports on the buying and selling of luxurious celebrity homes. It must have been the first time a Regional Mexican artist had been considered important enough to merit a mention in that section.

The February 7, 2009, *Los Angeles Times* article said: "When Latin music superstar Jenni Rivera moves, she moves fast. Rivera recently closed escrow in seven days on an Encino home she bought for 3.3 million. The 9,527-square-foot house she purchased is in a desirable neighborhood south of Ventura Boulevard. It has seven bedrooms and eleven bathrooms and was recently remodeled top to bottom. It sits on 4 acres and has a large grassy lawn, pool and entertainment patio that includes a spa and a waterfall. The home has marble and hardwood flooring, a gourmet kitchen, walls of windows and city lights views. There is a grand two-story entry, and the property is gated and private."

The piece noted that Rivera, 39, had been represented in the sale by Faby Llerandi of Divina Realty, her own real estate company. That was hardly surprising. By that time Jenni controlled every aspect of her business, from recordings, to tours, to real estate deals and everything else.

"I always wanted to be that way," Jenni responded in 2012 when I asked her if she had always been in control. "There were some arguments with my dad. My dad is my hero. He's a man who I admire and love very much. But I've always been so independent-minded that I wanted to do things my way, while my brothers did things my dad's way. I chose the songs and said, 'If you want me to record, dad, I'm going to choose the songs.' 'But I'm the executive producer and it's my label!' He said. 'Well, that's too bad, because I have to really feel what I'm going to sing.' And that's what I got used to, and I took that approach with the label where I've been now for over twelve years—Fonovisa, Universal. And they also trust me completely. They say: 'if it ain't broke, don't fix it.' They let me record what I want, they let me feel, they let the woman take charge of the artist, and that's really important. I've seen with the fans, the audience, that what they like the most is to feel it's a human being up there trying to connect with them, because one way or another when it's fake, I've seen so many times that it doesn't work. Whether it's with my label, with Mun2 or the radio, I always have the final say. I say I'm not controlling, but they would say I am," she said with a laugh. "I say it's the way to take care of what's mine."

In April 2009, at the *Billboard Latin Music Awards* Jenni won Top Album of the Year for a female artist. This significant award meant that she had been the top-selling female artist of the year, in any Latin music genre.

While she racked up one award after another on the way to superstardom, the media continuously tried to hype new stories around her: that a fan may have hit her, that Graciela Beltran said something to her, that her boyfriend uploaded a video on the Internet, and on and on. Jenni Rivera could appear on television every day, twenty-four hours a day, and they still wanted more: more scandals, but also more success and more awards. Everything that had to do with Jenni was endlessly fascinating. Her fans wanted to see her succeed, but they also just wanted to *see her*.

Yet somehow, Jenni managed to stay grounded. In terms of her family, she was in a wonderful place. She had her gorgeous house, where she lived together with all five of her children.

And nearby she had her parents, her brothers and her sister Rosie, all serving as a nurturing support system for Jenni.

In October 2009, Jenni, Don Pedro Rivera and Lupillo, Pedro Jr., Juan and Gustavo agreed to speak at the *Billboard* Regional Mexican Music Conference in Los Angeles. It was a historic event, the first time that all of the artists in the family would be on a single panel. That seminar was the second time Jenni had participated in a *Billboard* conference, sponsored by the magazine that covered the music industry and the artists who had the strongest effect on that industry. In 2007, as part of the *Billboard* Mexican Music Conference, Jenni had participated in a panel titled "Women in Mexican Music," along with Diana Reyes, Marisol and Vicky Terrazas (Horoscopos de Durango) and Graciela Beltran (yes, Graciela and Jenni were on the same panel, and both behaved as the consummate professionals that they were). The discussion was fascinating, as this group of highly successful women spoke frankly of the challenges they faced in a very male-dominated environment.

By 2009, Jenni had risen to new heights. Her career was climbing sharply, and she was invited to participate in the conference again, but this time on a panel called "The Rivera Dynasty."

"The Rivera family represents the essence of regional Mexican music and the Mexican community in the United States," said Gustavo Lopez, president of Fonovisa and Disa Records, the labels of Lupillo, Juan and Jenni at the time. "Their great musical talent combined with an excellent approach to business has made them—and they will continue to be—a powerful entity."

By then, the most powerful of them all was Jenni. She arrived at the panel wearing a tight but tasteful black wool skirt, with a black silk blouse. She wore her hair back and looked youthful, slender, beautiful, and exceedingly professional.

Jenni knew perfectly well how to play the role of "Diva" on stage, and the role of the serious career woman fully in control of her businesses off stage. In her interviews, Jenni always talked about her music, and her businesses with the same proprietary sense. In contrast with many other artists who preferred to keep their observations on a very superficial level, Jenni always liked to analyze her music, and herself, with the same objectivity. She was very clear that her success was no accident, nor was it simply the result of writing good songs and making good music, as many artists like to disingenuously say, as if millions of dollars had not been spent on marketing and promotion. Jenni talked openly about plans, projects, setting goals, and taking control. Together with her father and brothers, they all talked about their beginnings in the music business, their unity, and the importance of supporting each other as a family. It was an informative, and more than anything, highly emotional discussion, and Don Pedro wiped tears from his eyes more than once.

Around that time, Jenni was recording her album *La Gran Señora*, along with Jose Hernandez' mariachi band, Mariachi Sol de Mexico. It was her first album with a mariachi band, and she was extremely proud of this; not only because it was her first, but because at the time it was so rare to hear a female singer leading a mariachi band (and it still is).

Recording with a mariachi band presented a serious vocal challenge. Jenni had to take her voice to a new level. When we spoke about *La Gran Señora* on *Estudio Billboard* in 2010, Jenni sang songs live in the studio, accompanied by her guitarist. She was magnificent; even in that very intimate, acoustic setting, her voice was powerful and perfectly in tune, with that touch of bravura that mariachi music requires.

"Recording with a mariachi band was incredibly important to me, because I grew up with that," Jenni told me then. "That was the first music my ears ever heard, when I was in my crib. So I like it. If there's one thing I like to sing, it's mariachi. But after you start to work in one style, the record labels are very scared. They're afraid of artists going off recording in other styles, because they think they're going to lose the audience they have, or who knows what could happen. And with mariachi, for many years only the greats have been really successful at it. A Pepe [Aguilar], a Vicente [Fernandez], an Alejandro [Fernandez]; it's always been the same ones. It wasn't very commercial for new artists. Or for women."

But Jenni wasn't just any woman. In December 2009, *La Gran Señora* debuted at number 2 on the *Billboard* Top Latin Albums chart, and at number 1 on the Regional Mexican Albums chart, where it remained for four weeks. None of Jenni's albums had stayed in first place for so long up until then. Jenni's popularity continued to explode. Over the first six months of 2010, my production team and I tried many times to get Jenni on *Estudio Billboard*, the interview show with intimate acoustic musical performances that I host on the television network V-Me. Finally in August, we got the good news from Arturo Rivera, Jenni's publicist (who would also perish in the plane crash). Jenni could come to the *Estudio Billboard* studios in Mexico City on August 21. She would fly that same day from San Luis

Potosi, where she had a concert on August 20, and the next day she would fly out to Zacatecas, where she had another show. In other words, every minute of Jenni's days were carefully scheduled, her calendar was jammed.

On August 21, Jenni arrived at *Estudio Billboard* accompanied by her manager, her personal assistant and Arturo Rivera, a very small entourage for a star of her magnitude. With the schedule she was on, she must have been exhausted, but she did not show it, although she did seem somewhat reserved backstage, possibly because she didn't know what I was going to ask her. I went to see her in her dressing room to explain what we would talk about: her career, her music, her life, her songs. When she sat down next to me on the set, dressed for the interview in tight black pants, very high black heels, a low-cut black blouse under a leather jacket, and several bracelets and necklaces, Jenni was the diva. But over the course of the interview, Jenni never ceased being the open, honest woman she always was. It was one of the best interviews we ever had on *Estudio Billboard*, broken up with live performances of several of her songs, accompanied by her two guitar players, revealing notable musical maturity and depth.

"This mariachi album has been so important for me, I'll tell you why: it wasn't commercial for a woman to sing mariachi, and I was the executive producer and the musical producer, I chose one of the first songs called 'Ya lo se' [I already know]. It talks about the pain I feel when I find out my partner isn't coming back to me anymore," she said during the interview.

Jenni didn't specify who that partner may have been; if it was her ex-husband, Juan, whose death that summer had been incredibly painful for Jenni; or if it were one of the many stories her fans could identify with. What's certain is that by the end of 2009, something happened that was much more important than any record or any man. On November 19, at 6:29 in the morning, her daughter Jacquie gave birth to Jenni's first grandchild, a little girl, Jaylah Hope.

CHAPTER

17

New Hope

J enni loved her granddaughter Jaylah. She loved her with all her heart, and she shouted it to the four winds.

"Being a grandmother has been, I don't know, the biggest blessing of my life over the last few years," she told me on *Estudio Billboard*. "I'm so lucky to be a mother. I was a single mother for many years. I am a single mother now. I love my children. I adore them. Everything I am, I am because of them, they were what motivated me to fight for what we have now. But being a grandmother has brought me so much happiness. The happiness and joy is indescribable, knowing that little girl has my blood, but I'm not totally responsible for her. She has a mother. But I adore her. She's the light of my life right now."

A few years later, when she had launched her reality show "I Love Jenni" on Mun2, she devoted almost an entire episode to the dynamic between Jenni, Jaylah and Jacquie, showing just how close the bond was between Jaylah and Jenni, and how much the little girl resembled her grandmother. In that episode, Jenni is seen teaching Jaylah how to sing her songs, and how to move her arms in front of the television cameras. Jenni puts makeup on her, dresses her and fixes her hair. She is teaching her little granddaughter how to "be a diva," she tells her daughter Jacquie, who at the beginning looks on disapprovingly, but eventually she is won over by the scene's sweetness.

Jaylah's arrival was a real blessing for Jenni, in the wake of Juan's death. Aside from welcoming a new grandchild into her life, Jenni had found a new love. His name was Esteban Loaiza, and unlike her two ex-husbands Trino and Juan, he was famous; just as famous as Jenni even, but in a different field. Esteban was a professional baseball player, a pitcher who had played for the Chicago White Sox and the Los Angeles Dodgers. He was playing in Mexico when he met Jenni. Aside from their fame, they had other things in common: they had both been raised in California, but they both were closely connected with their Mexican roots; they both spoke Spanish and English; and they both came from humble families.

Jenni knew very well who Esteban was, because she was a big baseball fan, and she had seen him on television in 2003 when he pitched for the White Sox. Jenni wasn't aware that Esteban knew who she was, too. In a twist of fate, he came to see her in concert, not in Los Angeles but in Sinaloa.

"I was always a big baseball fan, but it wasn't until five years later, in 2008 in Mazatlan, Sinaloa, in December, that they told me he [Esteban] was playing with the Culiacan Tomateros, and he was there in Mazatlan," Jenni told Susana Heredia in an interview for *TVNotas*. "It was December 7, and I was going to perform. And he got in touch with my team and let them know that he was going to the show, he was bringing his mother, he was bringing his aunt, and they wanted to meet me. Even better if I said hello to them from the stage. So I did that."

The crowd in Mazatlan erupted when Jenni called Esteban up on stage, since he was a local hero in the area. As Jenni told Heredia in the interview: "He got up on stage and the crowd shouted, 'kiss, kiss,' and I'm all embarrassed, you can imagine, and then I took control of the situation and when he was walking off stage, he turned back and gave me a hug, congratulated me and went to leave. And I called for him from the microphone. I said, 'Hey,' and in front of five thousand people I said, 'these people want you to give me a baby.' And that was the hook," Jenni laughed.

And yes, that was the hook. Esteban and Jenni's relationship flourished throughout 2009, and on January 21, 2010, while they were out to dinner at a restaurant with Jenni's children, he asked her to marry him. Jenni cried tears of happiness. The date of Esteban's proposal was especially meaningful, since he had almost always worn number 21 on his baseball jersey throughout his career.

Several months later, in the fall of 2010, sitting next to his new wife on *Don Francisco Presenta*, Esteban would say what had attracted him to Jenni was her smile, her free spirit, and the things she said. For her part, Jenni admitted that at the beginning she had been attracted to Esteban physically, first and foremost: "He was tall, handsome, with a beard," she said to Don Francisco. "But after we talked all night, we spent two days talking, listening to music, walking on the beach, having dinner. I really got to know him: he's very down-to-earth, very generous. Generous with his time, and with me. You have to have a lot of patience to be with me."

In a home video that was shown on the program, Jenni was sitting next to Esteban at the restaurant when he took out a little box with the engagement ring in it and presented it to Jenni. She along with her children squealed with emotion, and off camera a voice could be heard saying, "Mom, give him an answer!"

"And obviously I said yes, and we got married on September 7 of this year," Jenni told Don Francisco.

It was a dream wedding, filled with family and celebrities, including Tito "El Bambino," a friend of Jenni's who sang at the reception.

"I never thought I would ever get married like a bride," Jenni said to Don Francisco. "I had never gotten married like that before. From the proposal down to all the details, my brother Pedro married us, surrounded by my brothers and sister, all my children, it was a very, very emotional day."

Listening to Jenni remember her wedding is very moving. Even though she had been married twice before and had five children, she had never had the wedding of her dreams. After so many problems and reversals, it seemed as if she had finally found true love, with someone who loved not only her, but her five children as well.

"I'm a woman who is very blessed by God," Jenni said to Don Francisco. "I have work, a successful career, and my brothers always said, 'all Jenni needs is a good man so she doesn't have to go through life alone with her children.' And my children are the most important thing to me, so it was really important to me that they accept Esteban."

With a stable, solid family dynamic, Jenni's life seemed to

have a newfound sense of calm. Her stardom kept right on grow-ing, but in a way, it seemed she was able to spend more time with her children.

"They are the light of my life and the reason so much has happened," Jenni candidly told Susana Heredia in her 2011 in-terview for *TVNotas*. "I started to fight and to live because of my first daughter, she was my first child. When my daughter was born I wanted to stay in school to give her a better life than what I had had, and to be a good example for her. My daughter has always been my right hand, my partner, and she's helped to raise my other children when I've had to travel, when I've had to rec-ord, when I've had to work."

Jenni was so proud of her children that she opened the door for them to be a part of her artistic life, if they wanted to. The first was, of course, the eldest, Chiquis.

CHAPTER 18

A Multimedia Career

J enni had been talking about working in television for years, and for at least the last five years she had been seriously considering a proposal to produce a reality show. But Jenni did not want to commit to it when her children were still small; it didn't seem right to put them on camera without their consent. So she waited until the moment was right.

"They were always asking me to do a reality show about my life, about what I do artistically, on tours, in recording sessions, during interviews," Jenni told me on *Estudio Billboard*. "But they always wanted to see the mother side of Jenni."

Jenni agreed to it—up to a point. In the summer of 2010, the bilingual television channel Mun2 began airing *Jenni Rivera Presents: Chiquis & Raq-C*, a reality show about two young Latinas in Los Angeles: Chiquis and her friend, the radio personality Raq-C (Raquel "Raq-C" Cordova). Jenni was the executive producer, but a big part of the show revealed the Diva at home with her family.

"I'm not totally out in front," Jenni told me on *Estudio Bill-*

board in the fall of 2010. "In some scenes I'm on camera, but usually I'm behind the cameras. And that's not weird for me. On the contrary, it's refreshing to see we're recording the ideas I have, and then decide what I want and what I don't want. It's another side of Jenni Rivera, the producer. It doesn't bother me. No, I like it; I like to see other people shine."

Jenni Rivera Presents: Chiquis & Raq-C debuted on July 3, 2010, at three o'clock in the afternoon. Even though the show centered around Chiquis and Raq-C, it offered a glimpse into parts of Jenni's life that her fans had never seen before: Jenni hanging out at home; Jenni the executive in her office, working side by side with Chiquis, her right hand; Jenni coming home, tired after playing countless shows on the road, greeted by her children and a home-cooked dinner for Mother's Day. The response on social media was immediate: the fans wanted more. More Jenni, who was irresistibly real. More Chiquis, who was beautiful, sweet, and bursting with personality.

The fans already knew that Jenni was Jenni. But if the show gave them one big surprise, it was Chiquis, who had her mother's charisma, an irresistible smile, and a sweetness that the television cameras captured incredibly well. Chiquis was a natural. That made Jenni's fans even more curious, and now they wanted to see the rest of her family. And Jenni responded.

The following year, she renegotiated her contract with Mun2 and returned with a new version of the show, this time called *I Love Jenni*. This new variation focused on the daily life of Jenni and her family: her five children, and her new husband, Esteban. Just like everything Jenni touched, the show turned to gold.

On March 5, 2011, at two o'clock in the afternoon, *I Love*

Jenni premiered on Mun2, and quickly became the channel's highest-rated show.

Many of the network's staff had expected it would be a big hit, but even so, Jenni's magnetic charisma was surprising. "Once the cameras started to role, our producer, a girl from New York, said, 'Oh my God, this woman is incredible.' You don't have to know her music to see she's a star," recalled Flavio Morales, the Senior Vice President of Programming and Production for Mun2, after Jenni's death. "Once the series started, the surprising thing was how consistent the ratings were, and the quality of the viewer it attracted. She attracted Latinas who had a higher income and were more bilingual than viewers of other shows we produced. And we could show Jenni: she was the mother who had to get up and take care of her children, even if she had only slept for two hours. Once she got to a meeting late, and it was because she had just come from the airport. She was a mom who worked. This was a show about a working mom."

Jenni's star power on television had been demonstrated before *I Love Jenni*. It was evident not only in the hundreds of interviews Jenni was constantly giving, but also when she was a judge on the 2001–2002 season of the show *Tengo Talento, Mucho Talento*, broadcast on Estrella TV. The Jenni of *Tengo Talento* was the singer, the diva, the star who many contestants would nervously ask if they could kiss on her cheek. Jenni always let them. Because on that show, more than anything she was their friend, their confidante, even their mom; a very sexy mom, to be sure, but still Jenni was able to form a meaningful relationship with the contestants, and everything she said was very important, and very entertaining.

I Love Jenni was entirely different. Since it was a reality show about Jenni and her kids, it included all of the members of Jenni's immediately family, but mainly it centered around Jenni (of course) and Chiquis. And someone new was added to the mix: by then Jenni had married Esteban Loaiza, and the baseball player had a kind of neutralizing effect on the family dynamics. Jenni's family was boisterous, active, and very talkative. Everything they did, they did big. In contrast, Esteban was calm, quiet, almost Zen.

In an interview with Latina.com in March 2011, Chiqui explained that her mom was very strong, and needed somebody who would balance her. She said Esteban was a calming influence, and a nice addition to the family because he let her mom be herself. If Jenni was in a bad mood, he would leave her alone. Chiqui said he was so centered and sure of himself, he would just tell Jenni her bad mood would pass, and when it did he would be there and she could come talk to him. He brought a lot of stability to their home, according to Chiquis, which was great.

As for the television show, Chiqui told Latina.com it was amazing because it's different. They weren't trying to be skinny little girls. They were big, they ate, and that's how they were—it was very real.

I Love Jenni was real in a very refreshing way. One day its star would appear in a dazzling gown, and the next in jeans with no makeup. Jenni boxed and tried to diet, she drank tequila on stage, and played with Jaylah. In a second-season episode, she wakes up in Los Angeles, exhausted, goes right to the airport in a sweat suit, headed to Miami for the *Billboard* Awards. When she gets there, she immediately transforms into the fabulous diva.

Everything that Jenni professed to be—a mother, business-woman, diva, singer, and just a real woman with a real woman's problems—all of those sides of her were revealed on the show, straight up. Jenni had always been real, but on *I Love Jenni*, all the walls came down; her fans had total access to her, and were invited into her home, her life, and her family. Even with all of that, it still wasn't enough. They still wanted more.

The first season of *I Love Jenni* was a stunning ratings success. So much so that in November 2011, Jenni signed a lucrative long-term contract with Mun2 to produce a series of shows, including the next seasons of *I Love Jenni*.

In a November 2011 *Billboard* interview, Pete Salgado, Jenni's manager and friend who coproduced *I Love Jenni* with her, said the deal with Mun2 was "a multimillion dollar commitment." "Jen's career has always been about breaking the barriers," Salgado said in the interview. "And I think we've accomplished that—a Mexican American family is just like the Kardashians. We just may eat different meals, but we're just as American as apple pie." As part of the deal, Jenni would also produce a new project for Chiquis: Chiquis N'Control.

"Mun2 has become a second home to me," Rivera said in a press release. "I'm glad to continue and grow our relationship and show mi vida loca—my life, my vision and feelings to my fans. I have built my career on honesty, reality and creating the most vibrant, impactful career for my fans and my family."

I Love Jenni would become the most successful original series Mun2 produced. "Jenni is an icon," Diana Mogollon, the General Manager of Mun2, said to *Billboard*. "She is one of the most respected and acclaimed Latinas in music and entertainment, and is an integral part of the Mun2 family. Jenni represents the vision of Mun2—cross-cultural, bilingual, influential and embodying the uniquely American lifestyle of our viewers."

Just as Jenni could appeal to a bilingual, bicultural audience, she could also reach an audience of monolingual English speakers, and an audience that exclusively spoke Spanish. She felt a special connection with this last group, and she always talked about it. They were like her. They were her people.

Jenni also had a major goal that she often spoke of: she wanted to be the Latina Oprah. Her ability to connect with the public was clear, but she wanted to take it to the next level. In October 2011, her radio show *Contacto directo con Jenni Rivera* began airing. On *Contacto directo*, which Jenni naturally produced herself, the Diva was at the microphone every Wednesday from ten in the morning until 2 in the afternoon, talking to her listeners. On one segment called "¿Qué haría Jenni?" [What would Jenni do?] she directly answered her fans' questions.

As with her television show, Jenni had been thinking about having her own radio show for years. The opportunity came to her from the Entravision network and its Vice President of Programming, Nestor Rocha.

"Nestor brought the Jenni concept to us," Jeffery Liberman, COO of Entravision told *Billboard*. "We had never done anything like it—not with a big star. She talked about her life, she took calls—almost all from other Latinas—she was an inspiration."

"She wanted to have that direct contact with her fans," Nestor Rocha told *Billboard* after Jenni's death. "Obviously you can't have that at a concert or on a prerecorded television show. Here she had that direct contact, and she could see exactly what her fans wanted. She wanted to talk to somebody. And she told her listeners everything that happened. She said, 'this is true, that's not true.'"

Jenni loved her radio show, and *I Love Jenni* filmed her a few times while she was doing the radio show, at least once with her sister Rosie at her side at the microphone.

At the *Billboard* Conference in 2012, Jenni talked about how her radio show gave her an opportunity to clear up any rumors. She said her fans wanted to listen to her version of events, to hear her talk about items in the news and gossip circulating about her.

For Jeff Liberman and his network, having Jenni on the air meant much more than simply having a star on their station. "We thought it was important to give Latinas in the United States a voice. No news station was focusing on that. And Jenni was very unique. Aside from being a Regional Mexican star and very different, what made Jenni particularly unique was with all she had—her television and radio shows and her companies—she never forgot about the U.S. Latina. And through her radio show, she was connecting with that Latina for four hours at a time. I don't see anybody else doing that."

Just as important, Jenni ran her radio show in the same way she managed her records, her music, her live concerts, and her television show: with 100% dedication, overseeing every single detail.

"I can't tell you how many hours Jenni spent going around with us to different advertisers to tell them about her vision for the show," Liberman told *Billboard*. "I'd say her desire to help, helped us sell the show [. . .] And I can't tell you how many times she was in Miami, for example, and the next morning she was with us. A lot of artists don't do that."

Jenni was perhaps the Diva of all divas. But she was always a diva with her feet planted firmly on the ground, and always strongly believed in the power and support of her fans and her people. For Jenni, unlike most female recording artists, being fabulous did not mean distancing yourself from the public. Just the opposite: the more fabulous, and more famous she was, the shorter the distance between her and her fans. And Jenni never, ever forgot where she came from.

On July 1, 2011, Jenni and her husband Esteban were each honored with a star on the Las Vegas Walk of Fame, making them only the second couple ever to have both received this (the first was Emilio and Gloria Estefan). The stars are made of granite, each weighing two hundred pounds, and were placed in the sidewalk on the Las Vegas Strip outside of the MGM Grand Hotel & Casino near other stars for such legends as Dean Martin, Elvis Presley and Frank Sinatra.

A few weeks later, on a sunny Tuesday afternoon, July 26, 2011, Jenni went back to her old high school, Long Beach Poly-technic, to receive a star on the Poly Walk of Fame. She was the fifth notable person to be honored by the school: some weeks before, the former mayor of Long Beach, Beverly O'Neill, the singer Thelma Houston, the former NFL football player Willie Brown and the tennis icon Billie Jean King had all been honored with their own stars.

Jenni attended the event wearing a white sundress with spaghetti straps, a big floppy brown sunhat, sunglasses and hoop earrings. She looked glamorous and beautiful. "This young lady is an inspiration," said City Councilman Dee Andrews as he called her to the podium.

Jenni stood behind the microphone, looking young and radiant, and said: "I was a nerd that played in the marching band on this same field, and I haven't been here since and it feels really good to be able to come back and . . . I would play my music then, and I came back because of my music and that feels really good. Thanks to all of you who have considered little ol' me from Long Beach, California for a star here at Poly High School, and thanks for remembering that I came out of here," she said, wiping away a tear, "I don't forget it. I'm still a Poly Jack Rabbit!"

Television, radio, stars. The year 2011 was a great one for Jenni. But it didn't stop there. That same year, Jenni Rivera took another big step in her career: she ventured into the movies.

CHAPTER 19

Jenni on the Big Screen

Jenni was a naturally entertaining artist, the kind who shines on camera and in any public appearance. In person, Jenni did not put on any diva airs, she did not go around surrounded by an entourage of dozens of people. She was always happy to say hi to her fans, and even hug and kiss them, she never refused a picture or turned down an interview. But on stage and in front of the cameras, Jenni transformed into a diva, in the best sense of the word; it was impossible to take your eyes off of her.

With her natural gifts, and her television show, and her audacious personality, willing to try anything, one would think Jenni would have tried acting much earlier. But it wasn't like that. Of all the different entertainment disciplines, that one did not grab her interest.

"Acting has never been my passion," Jenni said at the 2012 *Billboard* Conference. "I'm too lazy to repeat things. I get on stage, sing, sing my forty songs, they pay me and I leave. In acting you have to repeat one scene five, six, seven times."

But as Jenni continued working in all her different ventures, the legendary actor and director Edward James Olmos had his eye on her for a role in *Filly Brown*, a movie that his son Michael Olmos would direct, with Edward James Olmos serving as executive producer. And when Jenni was offered the part, even though she had never seriously considered acting, she couldn't dismiss it out of hand.

"I did it because Edward James Olmos called me up personally, and when you here that iconic voice, of this godfather of Latin Hollywood, then you think, 'He sees something in me that I don't see in myself.' And I thought I should try, so I did it."

But Edward James Olmos wasn't just any artist or personality. Like Jenni, he was from California—from Los Angeles—and just like Jenni, he was a Mexican American who had triumphed in spite of having few opportunities, with many factors working against him.

Jenni not only accepted the role, she took it very seriously, just as she approached everything she did. She spent a month rehearsing with her costars (one episode of *I Love Jenni* shows her taking an acting class), and she played a part of a woman who was very different from herself.

Filly Brown tells the story of "Majo" Tonorio, a young Los Angeles female rapper, in search of her voice and stardom, in spite of the many adversities she must overcome. Jenni plays the role of her drug-addicted mother, who is in jail, trying to maintain a relationship with her daughter from behind bars. Jenni also recorded a song, "Hurts So Bad," together with Olmos for the film's soundtrack.

Jenni was surprised when she saw herself on screen. "I couldn't believe a woman like me was up there, stripped down.

With no makeup, I was a *chola* in prison, with tattoos, drug addicted, everything that I'm not," Jenni remarked at the *Billboard* Conference. "And she was a bad mother. So for me, my greatest wish in life, my goal in life is to say that I could raise my children by myself and that I did a good job, to play that character who is nothing like me at all, I feel that it was an important achievement."

Jenni's part was emotionally powerful, but small. In fact, Jenni appears on screen for such a short time that Youssef Delara, the film's assistant director, didn't think she would take the part. And, as an independent production, *Filly Brown* could only pay the actors very little, just a few thousand dollars. "It was a lot to ask of a woman of her caliber," Delara told *The Los Angeles Times* in an interview on December 10, 2012. But as usual, Jenni did what she had been born to do. And without anyone's knowledge, Jenni asked the director to donate her salary to one of the photographers on-set, an older man who Jenni thought could use the money.

Filly Brown was a Sundance Film Festival selection, and debuted on hundreds of screens across the country in April 2013. For Olmos, who had been responsible for getting Jenni to play the role, the movie was just the start of what he thought would have been a great career for Jenni on the silver screen.

"Jenni was just an amazing force," Olmos said in an interview with *The Hollywood Reporter* after her death. "From the very beginning I've said that she could garner an Academy Award for her work in *Filly Brown*."

CHAPTER
20

The Greatest Stage

J enni's live performances were legendary. Her shows were long, and extremely elaborate, especially for a regional artist, with great attention to detail paid to the set, the lights, the video recording, and the wardrobe. Jenni could come out on stage dressed all in black—wearing a skirt or skintight jeans and high heels—throwing back a few drinks with her fans as she sang, her band behind her. Then came a mariachi set, and she would emerge wearing a gorgeous long dress, in vibrant colors, embroidered with flowers, and a long shawl draped around her shoulders.

But beyond how elaborately designed and visually beautiful they were, the main focus of her shows was her contact with the audience. Few pop artists let their fans get up on stage with them. Jenni not only allowed it, she encouraged it. Her fans came up on stage, hugged her, shared a drink with her. Going to one of her shows was like going to a fantastic party. And Jenni always put all of herself into every performance. She would play a Thursday night and give 110%. The next night, she'd do it again. She seemed to have endless emotional reserves.

"My shows are very emotional, very real," she said after her last concert in Monterrey. "So it's a lot of partying, a lot of fun. They pay me to entertain people who buy tickets to live the experience of seeing Jenni Rivera in concert. And that experience includes all that she is as an artist, and a woman. So I give all of myself. I'm very passionate. My fans as you can see are extremely passionate. Sentimental. They live my life. They know. I don't have to say anything to them, they are seeing me. [. . .] They come into my life, and as a singer I have to totally commit to what I'm doing to satisfy them."

Jenni was very consistent over the course of her career: consistent in her goals, in her philosophy, in her attitude. She always said the woman her fans saw up there on stage was really Jenni Rivera.

"At all of my shows I just want my fans to see the real me," Jenni said in an interview for *Radio al Aire* in 2003. "Not just the artist they see on television or in magazines, I want them to see me as a woman singing live, and get to know me a little better. Jenni Rivera the woman is almost the same as the artist. I'm a real person who has feelings just like my fans. I come from the *pueblo* and I'm for the *pueblo*, I'm from *la raza* and I'm for *la raza*. I'm not the other way around like a lot of artists who were born in a golden cradle and can't bring themselves down to the level of our people. I just sing, they pay me to sing but it's something I love to do, and I like to share it with the fans, and I want the fans to identify with me."

Jenni did a lot of things while she was up on stage. She sang. She raised a glass. She exchanged things with her fans: clothing, rings, dolls. The stories about Jenni's shows are legendary. She kissed her fans, laid down on the stage, once in Sonora she even took off her bra.

When she was asked on the television interview show *Aquí y Ahora* if she had had a few drinks before she did it, Jenni smiled good naturedly and said, "No, I was stone-cold sober. It was at a show in Sonora, and they started throwing bras on the stage, and they were all so little. And I said, just joking around, 'when one lands up here that's my size, I'll take mine off.' And that's what happened."

But Jenni did often drink at her shows—like she did in Monterrey—and she often made a toast with the first song. It was a part of the show, and part of what made her close with her fans; they raised a glass together. During the same interview, when she was asked if she drank alcohol during her shows, she replied: "Once someone asked me, 'Jenni, is it true you have a problem with alcohol?' and I said, 'No, we get along just fine!'"

The truth is Jenni didn't have a drinking problem. But she understood that having a drink on stage, together with her fans, was an essential ingredient to getting as close as possible to her audience.

The one quality that set Jenni apart from most other performers—male or female—was her ability to connect was so strong, and her fans were so loyal and so diverse, she could play in small arenas and nightclubs, and also perform in lavish theaters and concert halls, and sell them all out.

In the United States, Jenni was the first banda singer to sell out a show at the Gibson Amphitheatre, in 2006. She was the first Latina artist to sell out two nights at the Nokia Theatre in 2009; over 12,000 tickets were sold, grossing almost a million dollars, according to *Billboard* Boxscore, which tracks ticket sales. Jenni was also the first regional Mexican artist to play the Staples Center in Los Angeles, on September 3, 2011. Over 13,000 fans were at the show.

The writer Justino Aguila, who reviewed the concert for *Billboard*, wrote: "The American Dream arrived in long curly locks, 6-inch heels and a skintight turquoise-colored dress with an extended tail that flowed into white puffy ruffles behind the singer, Jenni Rivera."

She swept into the Staples Center that Saturday, full of surprises as the first female Mexican regional singer to ever have a show there, at the home of the Los Angeles Lakers. The more than 10,000 people who attended the concert were not just admirers of her music, but enraptured fans who hung on every note. They swooned, danced, yelled, and sang along to dozens of ballads about lost love, lying men, romantic escapades, survival, and strength.

That night, Jenni not only celebrated her fans, she celebrated a breathtaking career which was 100% of her own making. With that strong, constant bond that connected her to her fans, now she had become an artist with many years of experience, a singer with an angelic voice who had come very far, starting with one simple goal. She was accessible, strong, captivating, and spoke to a bicultural, bilingual audience that was also trying to realize the same dreams that she was. She was a wonderful role model, since she had managed to climb over obstacles in her way, and with her trademark bravado, she had become the greatest symbol of what you can achieve as long as you don't give up.

"'You could have been anywhere tonight, but you chose to be

here with me,' Jenni said to the audience. 'I know you could have paid bills with the money you spent for this concert, but you decided to be with me.' Rivera looked down. She took a deep breath and whispered, 'Thank you, thank you,'" Aguilar wrote in *Billboard*.

On December 9, 2012, when Lucero Amador interviewed her for the daily newspaper *La Opinion* and asked her what had been her greatest show, or if she still hadn't performed it, Jenni answered: "I definitely already had it. I think it was the concert at the Kodak Theatre [now the Dolby Theatre in Los Angeles] in 2005. Sold out. It was the first time I performed in a theater, in such a prestigious place, like that, where they hold the Oscars, where so many awards and honors have been given, so that meant so much to me."

Performing in these venues is a major achievement for any artist. They are the best stages for a show in Los Angeles, the entertainment capital of the world. For Jenni, it was doubly meaningful and important. She had grown up poor in Long Beach, a few minutes away from these places where generally pop stars, jazz performers or classical musicians performed, not regional Mexican singers. Setting foot on those grand stages was not just an honor, it also symbolized just how far Jenni Rivera had come.

CHAPTER
21

The Fashion Diva

The day before her death, Jenni performed in the Monterrey Arena, in a fabulous show with several wardrobe changes. Her most striking outfit was definitely a beautiful, bright fuchsia mermaid dress, with a yellow floral pattern running diagonally across Jenni's figure. The dress hugged her curves down to her knees, then opened up like a fan down to the floor. Jenni wore a yellow shawl that matched the color of the flowers in her dress—she wore many of her gowns with matching shawls—and during her performance, she would occasionally hold out her arms, letting the shawl fall around her sides, and she would spin, showing off the magnificently designed gown.

Her fans knew that when they went to hear Jenni sing at one of her shows, every time she sang *ranchera* music she would wear one of these spectacular dresses, often in a mermaid style with a floral design and matching shawl. They were designed by Adam Terriquez, a Mexican living in Huntington Park, California. For over ten years, he personally designed the most gorgeous gowns that Jenni wore in concert.

Terriquez was not just Jenni's designer, their relationship developed into a close friendship. They met in 2001 when Terriquez' brother, who was Jenni's makeup artist at the time, told him that Jenni wanted him to design a dress for her. "Jenni asked me to design a black dress for the Premios de la Radio that year, and we've been working together ever since . . . well, up until a few days ago, I was at her house taking measurements for other dresses," Terriquez said after his friend's death, still in disbelief.

When Terriquez began working with Jenni, he had already designed for big Mexican stars including Daniela Romo, Ana Barbara and Beatriz Adriana. He was known for his ball gowns with distinctly Mexican accents. In Jenni, he found a Los Angeles girl who liked to wear leather jackets and cowboy hats, but gradually she discovered glamour. Jenni would become his biggest client.

"For Jenni I'm designing a style more than fashion. Something that will last," Terriquez said in an interview on the morning show *Levántate*, where he talked about the dress he had designed for her to wear to the *Billboard* Mexican Music Awards. And that's how it was. Jenni's fans couldn't wait to see the dresses Terriquez designed for her. He estimated that he had designed around 500 dresses for her over the years.

What would come to define Jenni's style were the mermaid gowns Terriquez designed, which hugged her curves without revealing the love handles Jenni often complained about, and the butterfly dresses with the long, wide, draping sleeves that simulated the warrior butterfly that Jenni embodied. Jenni's favorite colors for her dresses, aside from red, were pink, turquoise, and coral.

"The first mermaid dress I designed was black with a floral pattern which she wore in concert at the Ford [Theatre] about ten years ago," Terriquez told Andrea Carrion in an interview for *Los Angeles Hoy* published on December 13, 2012. "I had warned her not to bend down, because the dress was really tight. At one point she bent down to hug a child, and from the balcony I could see her zipper in back came undone. Without missing a beat, she said right into the microphone, 'Where's my freakin' designer? Get out here and fix this dress!' Later, while she's still singing, I fixed the dress with some safety pins her mother had with her. When the show was over, she said cheerfully, 'Don't make my dresses with those cheap zippers anymore, buy the good ones.' That's how she was."

Jenni was constantly battling her weight, and always wanted to wear clothes that would make her look slender while showing off her curves. It was no accident that her dresses were almost always low-cut, and formfitting in the rear, a part of her body that she would complain about jokingly, but she also showed it off.

Terriquez remembered that Jenni's weight often went up and down. This is evident in her appearance over the years, and was a subject Jenni often talked about on her television show *I Love Jenni*. She was always going on a new diet, or trying to change her family's eating habits.

But Jenni had also learned to love her body, and was resigned to the fact that she would always be full-figured, a woman with large breasts and a generous backside, like so many other Latinas. For years she had tried to fit her body into the clothes, but finally she decided to fit her clothes to her body.

"We can't all be 36–24–36," she said to the magazine *Revista*

Mira in March 2005. "I like my big booty and having some meat on my bones. There's something to grab on to!"

In that same interview, Jenni mentioned that she was planning to launch her own clothing line in 2006, created especially for women like her, for her fans: "It's not easy to find sizes for full-figured gals like me, so I'll try to make the collection tailored for those women, and it will be very casual."

Jenni did not end up launching her clothing line in 2006, but she kept on working on it over the next few years, and—as with almost everything she said and thought—her goals and her statements on the project never changed. In April 2012, when I asked Jenni to speak at the *Billboard Latin Music Conference*, her clothing line was a subject of conversation again. She was especially excited about her new line of jeans, specifically designed for women who weren't a size 0 and who did have big rear ends that never looked good in most of the popular jeans out there on the racks.

"I want to dress women like me—not the mannequins in the stores because those clothes don't fit us," she said at the *Billboard* Conference, her words echoing what she had said six years before. "We're starting with the jeans. The jeans are for women with big hips and round butts. Because I'm so sick of going shopping and you try on jeans that are so low, if you sit down all your business is hanging out. You have to always readjust them. That's so annoying. I want jeans like my grandmother used to say they should be: that go up to your waist, fit well everywhere, without a roll spilling out here and another over there. I need that, and I know many of my Latina friends need the same thing."

Jenni launched her line of jeans in the spring of 2012, realizing a dream she had first had six years before. She promised that her customers would finally be able to look thinner, dissimulating certain love handles, or "lonjitas," as she called them, without showing any lines.

The jeans came in sizes 4–18, and cost $60, much less than other designer jeans. Jenni was very proud of them. She had designed something she herself could wear; as with everything she did, this was inspired by and was for her fans. If circumstances had been different, she probably would have introduced new items to the line in the coming years, but that was not to be.

J enni always said she was an entrepreneur more than a singer, and that outlook was reflected in her wardrobe. The times that I interviewed her on camera for *Billboard*, she always looked feminine and sexy, but also imminently professional. She liked to wear her high heels, either with skirts or pants, always with a jacket. For the last *Billboard* Conference, for example, she wore a formfitting purple dress under a jean jacket. She liked wearing purple, it gave her the air of an executive. Off camera and away from the limelight, she was much more casual, and was most comfortable in jeans, baseball caps and little makeup.

"My own personal style is very mixed," Jenni said on Batanga .com on March 3, 2005. "I like to dress in lots of different ways, and when I'm on stage, some people don't understand it; the people at my label don't understand it; they want me to dress, you know, like a regional Mexican artist, in jeans and leather and a cowboy hat. That's not me! That's not the person my fans have identified with. They want to know that Jenni can put on some dressy boots with a miniskirt and be in style, like they are. So, when I'm just relaxing, and I'm alone and no one's looking, I like to wear sweat suits and hip-hop style clothes—Adidas, Nike, sweat pants. I like that a lot, and I have a lot of sneakers. I like to dress like a businesswoman because that's how I started. I still like to do that. And when I go out, I put on a miniskirt and heels and look all sexy for the boys."

Jenni was very aware of the fact that she was a diva, and as such, she had to look absolutely magnificent on stage. For her last tour in Mexico, as always she asked Terriquez to design several dresses for the shows, and he fit her for them before she left. A week and a half before she flew to Mexico, Terriquez took fifteen dresses over to her house that she could bring to wear at her concerts.

"She had lost a lot of weight recently because she wanted to look good; she was crossing over into the English market and she wanted a different look," the designer recalled in an interview published in *Los Angeles Hoy* on December 13. "The last time I fitted her for a dress I said, 'You've lost a lot of weight.' She said, 'With everything that's going on, I'm losing weight without even going on a diet.' She was talking about the divorce. She didn't seem worried, but on the inside she wasn't doing so good."

That night out onstage in Monterrey Jenni looked beautiful. So beautiful that the image of her wearing that fuchsia dress would be seared in the memories of everyone there that night, and everyone who saw photos of her posted on the Web.

Days later, when rescue workers in Mexico were finally able

to locate the wreckage of the plane, one of the irrefutable signs that they had found her was that unmistakable fuchsia dress.

A day before it had represented Jenni Rivera's vitality, as she wore the bright dress on the stage and spun around and around, with the yellow shawl fanning out from her shoulders. Now the dress was by itself, tossed on the rocks like a rag, its bright color the only sign of life in those freezing, desolate mountains.

Billboard, La Voz and Other Glories of 2012

Two thousand twelve was an amazing year for Jenni. It started off on the right foot, as *Filly Brown* premiered at the Sundance Film Festival in January, and would open on screens across the country in April 2013.

In February came the Premios lo Nuestro, where Jenni won the award for Best Ranchero Artist of the Year, and for the sixth year in a row she took home the prize for Female Artist of the Year. She had first won that in 2007, when her music finally began to go into heavy rotation on the radio, and at the ceremony she had accepted her award wearing an elegant black dress.

In 2008, Jenni arrived at the Premios lo Nuestro with Esteban Loaiza, looking especially beautiful on the red carpet in a striking blue dress. That year Jenni was invited to sing on the show for the first time, and she appeared on stage in a Terriquez dress—a gorgeous gown with pink flowers and the trademark matching shawl—singing "Ya lo sé" accompanied by a mariachi band.

When she won Female Artist of the Year for the second time in a row, she dedicated the award to the most important man in her life: "Thanks to my fans who keep on voting for me, I love you guys. Thanks for sticking with me in good times and bad no matter what happens. I want to dedicate this award to someone very special. So much has happened since this man raised me and my brothers. This award is for my father; thank you for the music. I love you, Daddy. You're still my hero."

In 2011, Jenni won again, and sang again, this time performing "El," the theme song for the hit telenovela Eva Luna.

But in 2012 Jenni took a break from the Premios lo Nuestro. Although she won again, she could not attend the ceremony. Instead she attended the *Billboard* Awards to great fanfare a few months later.

She was invited to perform and also to participate in the *Billboard Latin Music Conference*. The conference usually has Q&A sessions with the biggest artists of the day, where they talk about their careers, their achievements and the industry. Q&A sessions in previous years had been done with Enrique Iglesias, Ricky Martin, Marc Anthony, Alejandro Sanz and Romeo Santos. In 2012, I invited Pitbull, Don Omar and Jenni Rivera, marking the first time a banda artist would have their own Q&A. The reasons for this were simple: Jenni was not only a star but a successful businesswoman, and conference attendees were interested in hearing about her career and her thoughts on the industry. That's what was described in the invitation that was sent to her manager Pete Salgado a few months before. And Jenni was a finalist for the *Billboard Latin Music Awards*; she would spend several days in Miami, in a very musical week. So Jenni decided to bring along a camera crew from *I Love Jenni* to follow her around for those three days in April 2012.

Months later, when the second season of *I Love Jenni* began airing on Mun2, an entire episode was dedicated to the *Billboard* Awards. It opens showing Jenni leaving her Los Angeles home, looking a little tired, like she would rather stay home with her children than have to go off and walk a red carpet. The cameras followed Jenni as she arrived at the airport in Miami, and later showed her rehearsing for her performance at the *Billboard* Awards at the Bank Atlantic Center at the University of Miami.

The next day, Jenni arrived for the Q&A session wearing a tight knee-length purple dress with a jean jacket over it. All of the editors of *Billboard* waited for her in a private area: I was there as the director of Latin content, along with my boss and the magazine's editorial director Bill Werde, and our publisher Tommy Page. A camera crew for *Billboard*.com was there too. Justino Aguila, another one of our Latin editors who had known Jenni for years, interviewed her backstage. As she usually was in these situations, Jenni was a little guarded at first, seeming to try to get a reading on what was happening. Unlike other artists who are very energetic and aggressive in interviews, in my experience with Jenni, she was professional and restrained above all. She was friendly and warm, but not especially effusive. That always would come later, when she felt more comfortable in her surroundings. One of the most gratifying things for a music journalist is following an artist from their beginnings all the way to superstardom. That happened to me with Jenni. I had been writing about her career since 2007, when she began climbing the *Billboard* charts. Now, seeing this strong, secure, motivated, hardworking and talented woman succeed on such a large scale made me feel so happy and proud.

My introduction that day said it all: "The most successful woman on the *Billboard* charts now."

Jenni strode into the conference room at the Marriot Marquis hotel in Miami to thunderous applause. I hugged her and showed her to her seat between Flavio Morales, of Mun2, and me; we would both be interviewing her.

"You got two of us now," I said jokingly, "We'll attack you from all sides!"

"I'm used to being attacked," she said with a smile, "It's okay."

"What do you want, Spanish or English?" I asked the audience.

"Español!" they shouted.

"You're in trouble," Jenni said, grinning. "Spanish, girl."

For the next hour, Jenni spoke with Flavio and me in Spanish, about her start in music, her father, her earliest recordings, her goals and achievements, her line of clothing, her companies, her fans and her family, her children, and her happiness as a mother.

She also talked about the book she was writing, which she had been talking about for years. "If I finish it in the next two months, I think I'll publish it at the end of this year," she said. "I think it will explain a lot of what has happened in Jenni Rivera's career. And maybe they can walk a mile in my shoes." When she died, Jenni had not yet finished the book, but she was close. It would be published in 2013.

Weeks later, when the episode of *I Love Jenni* aired, the things she said on camera really moved me. She said she had no idea it was going to be such an important event, with photographers and advertisers all over the place. It was a big deal. The media always wanted to write about gossip, she said, but at that conference people were really interested in the person. The interview made her think, and remember everything that had happened in her life, what she had achieved, and how she had gotten to where she was. It made her think about what she would do next. When people thought about Jenni Rivera, she said she wanted them to remember, if you struggle and something gets in your way every time, but you keep fighting anyway, then you can do it.

The following night, Jenni attended what would be her last *Premios Billboard* awards ceremony. In spite of her distaste for red carpets, at the very last minute she decided to walk it, and she looked very happy. She was especially beautiful in a long black gown and sparkling diamonds, with Esteban by her side.

Later I saw Jenni backstage, just about to go perform with her mariachi band, wearing a gorgeous red dress adorned with Swarovski jewels. She looked dazzling.

I n mid-2012, the producers of the television show *La Voz . . . Mexico* [The Voice . . . Mexico] began their search for new judges for their reality musical talent competition. The first season had featured Alejandro Sanz, Lucero, Espinoza Paz and Aleks Syntek. For the following season, the star-studded panel of judges would be made up of Paulina Rubio, Beto Cuevas, Miguel Bose and Jenni Rivera.

The problem was that Jenni Rivera didn't have time.

"You don't know how hard [the producers of] *La Voz . . . Mexico* fought to convince me," Jenni said in a 2012 interview with *La Opinion*. "We talked for months. I turned them down many times, I said that I couldn't be there on the dates they gave me because I had to throw a baby shower for my daughter-in-law, and a bachelorette party for my daughter getting married in September, and my daughter's fifteenth birthday party in October, the first time we would celebrate as a family. This is important to me. There's no show that could be more important than that. They had to move the dates around. I wasn't going to be a Miguel Bose who lives in Mexico for the duration of the show. I would be traveling. Those are sacrifices I have to make to fulfill my responsibilities as a mother, wife, and grandmother."

Jenni didn't like the idea of being away from home on Sundays—the day the show was recorded—which was usually a day she liked to spend with her family, as long as she didn't have a show. But, in the end, she let them talk her into it. And she loved it. "It's been such a wonderful experience. And I've won a lot of new fans," she said at her press conference in Monterrey. "Before my shows would sell out, but now they sell out in advance. And the people knew me through my music, but they didn't know how I talk, how I am."

We should remember that even though she was the "Diva de la Banda," Jenni didn't have the same track record in Mexico as, say, her brother Lupillo did. She had begun making serious inroads into Mexico five years earlier, and now she was a star. But not on the same level as she was in the United States.

With the release of *La Gran Señora* in 2009, the eighth of her career, she planned a more comprehensive strategy. This was the first album she sang with a mariachi band from start to finish, placing her on another musical and artistic level. Now Jenni wasn't just a banda singer. She was a voice. And to underscore this, she recorded a concert for the Televisa network, and the Mexican public began to get to know her better.

The major breakthrough came with *Joyas prestadas* in 2011, with her interpretations of banda and pop songs, which allowed the album to get radio play on two types of stations: pop radio, and Mexican radio. *Joyas prestadas* was a collection of cover songs first made famous by other female singers—hence the title, "borrowed jewels," in English—on which Jenni paid tribute to those singers who had so strongly influenced her career, including many of the artists whose records she had listened to at the flea markets, while she sold her father's records.

"What happened was that around 2010, my Twitter fans were saying that another female artist was criticizing me for always recording all covers, and what a joke, that kind of thing," Jenni said at the *Billboard* Conference. "And they said, 'We want a new record so no other artist can criticize you.' And then just to play devil's advocate, I gathered together all my favorite songs from artists like Isabel Pantoja, Ednita Nazario, Rocio Durcal, and I said, 'Just for spite I'm going to record all the songs of theirs that I like.' And what a great impulse because in Mexico it's double platinum."

The most challenging thing about the album, Jenni explained, was that her label wanted her to record pop versions of some of the songs. "These were the songs I played on the tape player when we had the little stand at the flea market, and I wanted to attract customers. So I would play this music, and it has a special place in my heart, I have very fond memories. It was very hard for me to cut songs. So I said: 'Why don't I record a banda record, and a pop record, and see what happens.'"

Joyas prestadas was released as a banda album and a separate *ranchera* album. Both were successes. "We had an incredible success," Victor Gonzalez, the president of Universal Music Latin Entertainment (UMLE) told *Billboard*. "More than anything the repertoire she selected was very important, because she had songs [by such artists] as Rocio Durcal, which put her in a place where she was paying tribute to these women, but the people recognized her talent, too. And that was when we broke Mexico."

Jenni started appearing on the radio and sales charts in Mexico, reaching number one in sales for the record store chain Mix-Up. It was a huge hit. *Joyas prestadas* flew off the shelves, and it was suggested that Jenni be a judge on *La Voz*. Once she agreed to do it, and once the show started airing, the reaction was immediate.

"We have done some surveys on *La Voz*, Web surveys asking how the people feel and think, and Jenni got their attention right away," Gonzalez said to *Billboard*. "People that know her fall in love with her."

They fell in love because Jenni was Jenni. And Televisa let her just be herself.

"I can be kooky or silly, or sensitive or spontaneous," Jenni said in her last press conference in Monterrey after her concert. "I want to be real, I want to be authentic for my fans. They never censure me. They let the cameras roll. But I am who I am."

For Jenni, it was also meaningful and fun to pal around with people on the level of Miguel Bose, whose records she sold at the flea markets when she was a kid.

As *La Voz* was up and running, Jenni kept moving ahead on all fronts. In March, Jenni had signed with Creative Artists

Agency (CAA), the prestigious talent agency representing actors, singers, athletes, and other celebrities in Los Angeles. Although other agencies had tried to woo Jenni before, they had mainly been interested in her tours, the most lucrative part of her business. But CAA saw great potential in Jenni as a personality, and they began talking about how to cross her over to the general market, in English.

The agents at CAA spent a lot of time with Jenni. They went to her concerts, and watched her work on her many companies. They assigned a producer and a writer to her, and rolled up their sleeves. After a while, they had a television pilot ready, and presented it to the major networks. They all made offers. Jenni chose ABC, and in November 2012 she signed a contract to star in a comedy series called, simply, "Jenni."

"[The character] Jenni is a single mom with three sons and a daughter, and she and her husband separated because he was an alcoholic and she couldn't have that kind of example in their home," Jenni said after the show in Monterrey. "Jenni's father passes away, and she inherits a bar, with all its problems and debts, and I have to work in that bar. I have a married sister with a really sexist husband, I'm always fighting with her. All the guys who want to date her come around the bar. I think one of the potential boyfriends is African American, which would be great," she said to the Mexican reporters with a smile. "I'm going to sing once in a while. I never thought I'd be a singer," Jenni added, thoughtful. "By some fluke I became a singer, and I never thought everything that has happened in my career as an artist would happen. And I've never wanted to be an actress. Now when they say, 'Jenni, you're the first Latina actress to star in an

American TV show,' just imagine. They are such big blessings I never expected, which would completely change my life."

Consider for a moment what could have happened if Jenni had produced her show on a major American network. A Latina had never been in that position before. Sofia Vergara was a phenomenon on *Modern Family*, but she wasn't the star of the series, which has an ensemble cast. Still, Vergara's success underscores the possibilities that Jenni had, after already testing the waters with *I Love Jenni*. With her experience, charisma and huge fan base, I'm sure her show would have been a tremendous success, and could have opened up new worlds of possibilities for other Hispanic stars.

As if everything she had already experienced in 2012 weren't enough, there were more blessings in store, which were the most important of all for Jenni. On August 28, Jenni's second granddaughter was born, Luna Amira Marin Ibarra, her twenty-year-old son Michael's first child with his girlfriend. On April 3, Jenicka turned fifteen and Jenni was able to throw her a fabulous *quinceañera* to celebrate.

And in November, Jacqui, the mother of Jenni's first grandchild Jaylah Hope, married Miko Campos, in a wedding that was a televised special for Mun2. *Jenni Rivera Presents: My Daughter's Wedding* was a ratings success, as the most-watched show on television for Latinos between eighteen and forty-nine years old.

But in spite of all the triumphs and joys, not everything was picture perfect for Jenni in late 2012. In April, she had attended the *Billboard* Awards on her husband Esteban's arm, and could not have looked any happier or more radiant. On the red carpet, as she played the "artist," she turned every now and then to look back fondly at her man, waiting for her patiently as she did her work. He was strong, tolerant, calm, and as famous as she was though in a different field, he understood her and supported her. They really looked like the perfect couple. Until October 3, 2012, when Jenni wrote an open letter to the press:

> *Friends in the press, first let me thank you for the support you have always given us and in this case in particular for JENNI RIVERA in her career, we want to let you know in order to avoid negative comments and speculation, that the story that JENNI began in December 2008 with professional baseball player Esteban Loaiza and whom she married on September 8, 2010, sadly came to a definitive end on Monday (October 1). Divorce papers were filed citing irreconcilable differences on behalf of both parties stemming from private circumstances that occurred over the course of their two-year marriage, and those circumstances are private for them both and will not be made public.*
>
> *Making this decision has not been easy, but considering her own well-being and that of her children, her family projects, her careers as a businesswoman, singer and artist, JENNI knows she needs to have a balanced, peaceful life, and with that in mind made the decision to separate from Esteban.*

Jenni never gave specific reasons for why she was divorcing Esteban after two years of what seemed like an ideal marriage. In an in-depth interview on *El Gordo y La Flaca*, Jenni would only say that "finding out about a person's certain activities is enough to make the decision that I did." There was no fighting, or abuse, or third person. She would only say that on September 21, she found out about some things that she could not tolerate. On October 2, Jenni filed for divorce. There was no possibility of reconciliation, according to Jenni.

Ever the optimist, Jenni said, "I believe in marriage, I believe in love, I think Jenni can fall in love with a man who loves and respects me like I deserve. I have to keep on inspiring myself and I can't let this defeat me. Do I believe in love? Of course I believe in love."

It wasn't easy for Jenni. On television she looked sad and disillusioned. But she kept on working, and kept on appearing on *La Voz* week after week. Watching her popularity grow, Universal asked Jenni for a new record. But Jenni didn't have time to record a whole new album. So she selected some of her greatest hits and released a compilation *La Misma Gran Señora*. It included a new song of the same title, and as with so many of Jenni's songs, it was a tribute to a woman who others keep trying to drag down, but she manages to forge ahead. Some of the lyrics say: "Without you I'll still be the same great lady/without me, you're worth nothing after today."

La misma Gran Señora was first released in Mexico, to take advantage of Jenni's exploding popularity thanks to her role as a judge on *La Voz*. In the United States, in an uncanny twist of fate it was scheduled to be released on December 11, 2012, and it was.

On December 8, 2012, Jenni Rivera arrived in Monterrey to play a show in the Monterrey Arena. The concert had been sold out for weeks. Jenni arrived in the afternoon, followed shortly after by her band, her mariachi band and her production team, who were traveling from Colima where they had played a show the night before. The *I Love Jenni* production team also came along, an unusual occurrence, as they had filmed the show in Colima. Jenni had talked about showing her fans what being a touring performer was really like for the third season of her reality show, which they had already begun filming. She wanted viewers to see not just Jenni the mother, but Jenni the working artist.

The performance in Monterrey lasted for hours, as Jenni's shows always did. She sang, cried, drank, and partied. Right after the show, in the early hours of the morning, she gave a long press conference which seemed more like a confessional.

"Blessed," she responded simply when a journalist asked how she was feeling. "The best way I can describe how I feel is blessed, very lucky, very loved. A lot of times I can't believe the things that happen in my professional life—well, in my personal life too—but I feel really blessed."

At the end of the night, she was asked again how she was doing, and she answered with her trademark honesty that made her so special: "Oh, I'm so happy. Yeah, some really heavy things have happened in my life, but I can't, I can't get hung up on it. I can't just think about the negative because that drags you down, that destroys you. I have children, and grandchildren, and parents, and brothers and a sister, I have fans waiting for me. Maybe I'm trying to push all the problems away and focus on the positive, and that's the best I can do."

Jenni finished her press conference, and instead of heading to her hotel, as had been previously planned, she went straight to the airport to board a private jet bound for Mexico City.

The blurred images of Jenni wearing a green sweat suit and leaving the small airport are the last images we have of her.

Days later, the site of the plane crash would be found. Lying among the wreckage was the Terriquez pink floral dress, still as vibrant as its owner, a mute testament to the glory, now lost, and sadness of so many brilliant plans in the works for a dazzling future, now tragically cut short.

"There are offers for more movies, and there has always been talk about the movie version of my life," Jenni said back in April, when we asked her what she had planned for 2013. "We'll see what happens after the book. Because what I'm doing already is enough, but maybe there will be some change in my career, a change in my life in general. Since that calendar says everything's going to end at the end of 2012; that can mean different things for different people. Maybe something in my life will end then, and something will start in a new area."

Jenni Rivera's Legacy

After Jenni Rivera's death, many comparisons have been drawn between her and Selena, the Tejana singer who also died tragically young. But the real similarities between the two women have more to do with personal qualities than the fact that they both suffered early deaths. Like Selena, Jenni had been one of the few successful faces and voices that the very large population of Mexican American women in the United States could identify with. They identified with both women's stories, their backgrounds, their families, even their physical appearance. Finally, there was someone successful who looked like them. The inspirational impact these two cultural icons had cannot be overstated.

In the United States, Mexican culture is imported from Mexico, and arrives prepackaged and homogenized. I would venture to say that it would have been more work for Jenni to have reached the level of success she did if her career had started off in Mexico, where her image, her attitude and her casual outspokenness clashed with accepted norms.

During an interview with *TVNotas* in 2011, Jenni was asked if she considered herself a sex symbol, a question that made her laugh: "I've never thought that. To me, sex symbols are Maribel Guardia, Ninel Conde, I admire them so much for their beauty. I'm just a woman, a singer that some people think about having sex with. I don't know," she laughed.

Maybe Jenni didn't think of herself as a sex symbol, but she was. She was a sex symbol, and more than that she was a symbol of everything that was possible, even coming from a very disadvantaged background. She symbolized the importance of family, and a family's roots, and that being and acting Latino can be an advantage, not always an obstacle to overcome.

At the moment of her death on December 9, at only forty-three, Jenni was at the height of her career. Over the mere thirteen years since she had started out in music, she had become the highest-selling female artist in regional Mexican music, and she was a formidable business impresario with several successful companies in her empire: a cosmetics line, a line of hair care products, her clothing line, her radio show, her television reality show, and her foundation. The icing on the cake would have been the contract she signed with the ABC network one week before her death: Jenni was to star in her own television series, in English, in primetime. That would have made her the only Latina—yes, the *only* one—to star in her own television series, bearing her name.

Jenni's success in multiple platforms was so great that when her flight's disappearance was made public on December 9, 2012, her name became a "trending topic" on Twitter. Within forty-eight hours, Jenni Rivera—regional Mexican music star, beloved diva of Latina women in the United States, and icon in Mexico—became a global superstar. Media outlets in languages other than Spanish that had never written one word on Jenni Rivera rushed to tell the story of the daughter of humble Mexican immigrants who had become a diva in her own right. Her name went all around the world in a matter of hours. Jenni Rivera had become a worldwide superstar overnight.

This doesn't happen just because someone dies tragically. Sudden deaths of well-known people do generate interest, but not to this extent, or for this length of time. Jenni was such a fascinating, magnetic person, with such an amazing career, and she was such a creative powerhouse musically, her death simply opened the world's eyes to the very high level of stardom she had already achieved and so rightly deserved, and propelled her to an even higher place.

On leaving this world, Jenni has left behind a great artistic legacy. She recorded almost twenty studio albums, in a variety of genres: banda, *ranchera* and pop. She filmed two seasons of *I Love Jenni*, with another in progress. She leaves her lines of makeup, clothing and her signature fragrance. She leaves her foundation, with her sister Rosie at the helm, which was beginning to soar, performing such important work that positively affected so many. She also leaves the book she had begun writing, which would be published in 2013.

But even more importantly, she leaves behind her children, who seem to have inherited their mother's perseverance, optimism and groundedness. She leaves her two grandchildren and the whole Rivera family, who will no doubt work to carry on her legacy, and keep her name alive for generations to come.

Jenni Rivera was irresistibly real. Curvaceous, honest and utterly unpretentious, a diva but extremely accessible and open. From very early on in her career, Jenni had it very clear in her own mind that the person she was in her daily life was the same person she would be as an artist.

"I am a real woman who sings about what I live," she said on more than one occasion. "And more than anything, I'm a mom."

Who was Jenni Rivera?

Like few others in the entertainment world, Jenni personified the American Dream. Born in the United States, but raised as a Mexican, bilingual and bicultural, she was the face of her fan base, the large community of Mexican American women who have never seen themselves represented in the media. She was that woman, that friend, that mom, that sister who had grown up in the barrio, far away from the excess and luxuries of America's middle class. She was the fighter, the teen who got pregnant and instead of celebrating her *quinceañera* or "sweet fifteen," she had a daughter; she graduated from high school at the top of her class in spite of all the daunting obstacles standing in her way; she went to college and did what she had to do to raise her children, without asking for anything from anyone.

Latinas in the United States watch Spanish-language television, but rarely see themselves reflected in the thin, blonde, model-gorgeous actresses that dominate the screen. In Jenni, they did see themselves. Jenni was them, with the same face, and dreams, and reality. She understood their struggles, their financial problems, their cheating men, their tears. She sang about their lives — about the lowlife men, the corner bar, the best girlfriends, the parties, the other women, the wives — and she lived their lives.

While most artists try to run away from their pasts and reinvent themselves, the more famous she got, the prouder Jenni was of her background and of who she was.

Single mother. Domestic violence survivor. Grandmother. Friend. Fighter. Winner.

La Reina de las Reinas—the Queen of Queens.

Acknowledgments

To Jenni Rivera, the inspiration for this work. To my incredible literary agent, Aleyso Bridger, and to Erik Riesenberg and Carlos Azula of C. A. Press/Penguin, for giving me the opportunity to write about one of the most fascinating women in entertainment.

To *Billboard* for their support.

And to Jenni Rivera's family and friends.

Jenni Rivera's Discography

SOMOS RIVERA (1992)

1. Somos Rivera
2. Alma enamorada
3. Amor prohibido
4. Juan Guardado
5. Me espera el camino
6. De visita al mundo
7. Recuerdos de Culiacán
8. Cuento perdido
9. Magda Otilia
10. Antojos nobles

POR UN AMOR (1994)

1. Por un amor
2. Esperando que me quieras
3. Collar de penas
4. Tengo miedo
5. Soy madre soltera
6. Trono caído
7. Estados que quiero
8. El viejo y yo

9. Una estrella lejana
10. Marisela y Chalino
11. Viejo vaquetón
12. Así soy yo

LA CHACALOSA (1995)

1. La Chacalosa
2. También las mujeres pueden
3. Libro abierto
4. Cruz de madera
5. Embárgame a mí
6. Por una rencilla vieja
7. Si tú pensabas
8. La perra contrabandista
9. Cuando el destino
10. Mi gusto es
11. Ni me debes ni te debo

JENNI RIVERA Y SUS MEJORES 17 ÉXITOS (1995)

1. Adiós a Selena
2. Poco a poco
3. La novia del plebe
4. Embárgame a mí
5. Los dos amantes
6. Por un amor
7. Se me cierra el mundo
8. Libro abierto
9. Si tu pensabas
10. Somos Rivera
11. Amor prohibido
12. La Chacalosa
13. También las mujeres pueden

14. Recuerdos de Selena
15. El columpio
16. Para un gran señor
17. Ni cura ni juez

REINA DE REINAS (1999)

1. Reina de reinas
2. El desquite
3. El orgullo de mi padre
4. Popurrí de chelo
5. Los traficantes
6. La reina es el rey
7. La Martina
8. El bato gacho
9. La maestra del contrabando
10. Salúdame a la tuya
11. Las cachanillas

SI QUIERES VERME LLORAR (1999)

1. Brincos dieras
2. Perdonar es olvidar
3. Llanto rojo
4. Lágrimas, sudor y sangre
5. La puerta de Alcalá
6. Si quieres verme llorar
7. Vivir sin tu cariño (*Without You*)
8. Nosotros
9. Cómo vivir sin verte (*How Do I Live*)
10. Tonto
11. Yo te agradezco

QUE ME ENTIERREN CON LA BANDA (2000)

1. Que me entierren con la banda
2. Como tú decidas
3. Que un rayo te la parta
4. La reina del palenque
5. Son habladas
6. Ni estando loca
7. Mañana (te acordarás)
8. Solo sé de amor
9. Sinaloa… Princesa norteña
10. Rosita Alvirez
11. Las malandrinas (corrido en vivo)

DÉJATE AMAR (2001)

1. Una noche me embriagué
2. Déjate amar
3. Mi vida loca
4. Querida socia
5. Y te me vas
6. Madre soltera
7. El último adiós
8. Agente de ventas
9. Cuando yo quiera has de volver
10. *Wasted Days and Wasted Nights*

SE LAS VOY A DAR A OTRO (2001)

1. *Angel Baby*
2. No vas a jugar
3. Cuando abras los ojos
4. El nopal
5. Tristeza pasajera

6. Chicana jalisciense
7. Ni tu esposa, ni tu amante, ni tu amiga
8. Se las voy a dar a otro
9. Se marchó
10. Escándalo

20 EXITAZOS CON LA DINASTÍA RIVERA (2001)

1. El moreño (cantado por Lupillo Rivera)
2. Cruz de madera (cantado por Juan Rivera)
3. Reina de reinas (cantado por Jenni Rivera)
4. Valientes reconocidos (cantado por Gustavo Rivera)
5. Mi casita blanca (cantado por Lupillo Rivera)
6. Los atizados (cantado por Juan Rivera)
7. También las mujeres pueden (cantado por Jenni Rivera)
8. El recreo (cantado por Juan Rivera)
9. Perico, vino y cerveza (cantado por Gustavo Rivera)
10. La Martina (cantado por Jenni Rivera)
11. El avionazo (cantado por Lupillo Rivera)
12. Que me fusilen (cantado por Juan Rivera)
13. La Chacalosa (cantado por Jenni Rivera)
14. La balanza (cantado por Gustavo Rivera)
15. Tú y las nubes (cantado por Lupillo Rivera)
16. El día del contrabandista (cantado por Juan Rivera)
17. La vida prestada (cantado por Jenni Rivera)
18. La captura de Mayel Higuera (cantado por Juan Rivera)
19. El desquite (cantado por Jenni Rivera)
20. Me dicen El Chivo (cantado por Lupillo Rivera)

HOMENAJE A LAS GRANDES (2003)

1. La papa sin catsup
2. A escondidas
3. Por un amor

4. Ese hombre
5. Juro que nunca volveré
6. La tequilera
7. Ahora vengo a verte
8. Hacer el amor con otro
9. Homenaje a mi madre
10. *Where Did Our Love Go*
11. La papa sin catsup (versión norteña)
12. A escondidas (versión norteña)
13. Juro que nunca volveré (versión norteña)
14. Hacer el amor con otro (versión norteña)

DINASTÍA RIVERA VOL. 3 (2003)

1. Sin fortuna (cantado por Lupillo Rivera)
2. Una botella (cantado por Juan Rivera)
3. El malquerido (cantado por Gustavo Rivera)
4. El bato gacho (cantado por Jenni Rivera)
5. Vengo a verte (cantado por Lupillo Rivera)
6. Si las nubes (cantado por Juan Rivera)
7. El gavilán pollero (cantado por Gustavo Rivera)
8. Salúdame a la tuya (cantado por Jenni Rivera)
9. 20 Mujeres – en vivo (cantado por Lupillo Rivera)
10. El rebelde (cantado por Juan Rivera)
11. El primer tonto (cantado por Gustavo Rivera)
12. Otra herida más (cantado por Juan Rivera)
13. Los traficantes (cantado por Jenni Rivera)
14. Tu cabeza en mi hombro (cantado por Gustavo Rivera)
15. La Reina es el Rey (cantado por Jenni Rivera)
16. Sufriendo a solas (cantado por Lupillo Rivera)
17. Ando que me lleva (cantado por Juan Rivera)
18. Que vuelva conmigo (cantado por Gustavo Rivera)
19. Brincos dieras (cantado por Jenni Rivera)
20. México lindo y querido en vivo (cantado por Lupillo Rivera)

SIMPLEMENTE LA MEJOR (2004)

1. Querida socia
2. Las malandrinas
3. Se las voy a dar a otro
4. Cuando abras los ojos
5. Chicana jalisciense
6. Que me entierren con la banda
7. Se marchó
8. Mi vida loca
9. Tristeza pasajera (ilusión pasajera)
10. *Angel Baby*
11. Reina de reinas
12. La Chacalosa
13. Las mismas costumbres
14. Amiga si lo ves
15. Simplemente la mejor
16. Las mismas costumbres (versión norteña)
17. Amiga si lo ves (versión norteña)
18. Amiga si lo ves (versión pop)

PARRANDERA, REBELDE Y ATREVIDA (2005)

1. Parrandera, rebelde y atrevida
2. Qué me vas a dar
3. De contrabando
4. Brincos dieras
5. La mentada contestada
6. No vas a creer
7. Imbécil
8. No me pregunten por él
9. Qué se te olvidó
10. Jefa de jefas

11. Me siento libre
12. Cuando muere una dama (La Golondrina)

DINASTÍA RIVERA (2005)

1. El albañil (cantado por Lupillo Rivera)
2. El gallo de San Juan (cantado por Lupillo Rivera)
3. Cielo azul, cielo nublado (cantado por Lupillo Rivera)
4. Y ándale (cantado por Lupillo Rivera)
5. Mi despedida (cantado por Lupillo Rivera)
6. La papa sin catsup (cantado por Jenni Rivera)
7. Querida socia (cantado por Jenni Rivera)
8. Una noche me embriagué (cantado por Jenni Rivera)
9. Dame por muerto (cantado por Pedro Rivera)
10. Corrido de Chihuahua (cantado por Pedro Rivera)
11. El abandonado (cantado por Juan Rivera)
12. Mi último deseo (cantado por Juan Rivera)
13. Qué suerte la mía (cantado por Gustavo Rivera)
14. Anhelo (cantado por Gustavo Rivera)

Bonus track
Qué te ha dado esa mujer – en vivo, (cantado por Lupillo a dúo con Pedro)

EN VIVO DESDE HOLLYWOOD (2006)

1. Parrandera, rebelde y atrevida
2. La Chacalosa
3. Popurri: Reina de reinas/Rosita Alvirez/Mi vida loca
4. Las malandrinas
5. Popurri: Como tú decidas/Cuando yo quiera has de volver
6. Popurri: *Wasted Days & Wasted Nights/Angel Baby*
7. Chicana jalisciense
8. Se marchó

9. Se las voy a dar a otro
10. Cuando abras los ojos
11. El nopal
12. Popurri: A escondidas/Hacer el amor con otro

BESOS Y COPAS DESDE HOLLYWOOD (2006)

1. Por un amor/Cucurrucucú paloma
2. Juro que nunca volveré
3. Querida socia
4. Soy madre soltera
5. La tequilera
6. Homenaje a mi madre
7. Cuando yo quería ser grande
8. Las mismas costumbres
9. Amiga si lo ves
10. Qué se te olvidó
11. Qué me vas a dar

Bonus tracks
12. Besos y copas
13. Mil heridas

MI VIDA LOCA (2007)

1. Intro: Escúchame
2. Mi vida loca 2
3. Intro: Mi primer amor
4. Ahora que estuviste lejos
5. Intro: *Look At Me Now*
6. Mírame
7. Intro: Nuestro padre
8. Sangre de indio
9. Intro: Qué bonito se siente

10. La sopa del bebe
11. Intro: La manutención
12. Cuánto te debo
13. Intro: Equivocada
14. *I Will Survive*
15. Intro: Mi madre y yo
16. Déjame vivir - Vicente Uvalle
17. Intro: Mis hermanos y yo
18. Hermano amigo
19. Intro: Yo era su reina
20. Dama divina
21. Intro: Pimienta y especies
22. Inolvidable
23. Intro: Madre y padre
24. Sin capitán
25. Intro: Metamorfosis
26. Mariposa de barrio
27. Gracias… mi GENTE

LA DIVA EN VIVO (2007)

1. Sufriendo a solas
2. Popurrí: Por un amor/Cucurrucucú paloma
3. La diferencia
4. Inocente pobre amiga
5. Paloma negra
6. Libro abierto
7. Me siento libre
8. Brincos dieras
9. Qué me vas a dar
10. De contrabando
11. La mentada contestada
12. Navidad sin ti

JENNI (2008)

1. Chuper amigos
2. Culpable o inocente (versión álbum)
3. Envuélvete
4. Tu camisa puesta
5. Ni me viene ni me va
6. Con él
7. Cuando me acuerdo de ti
8. Fraude
9. Trono caído
10. Vale la pena
11. La cama
12. Mudanzas
13. Culpable o inocente (versión pop)

LA GRAN SEÑORA (2009)

1. Yo soy una mujer
2. Por qué no le calas
3. Estaré contigo cuando triste estés (*Before The Next Teardrop Falls*) (versión original)
4. Déjame volver contigo
5. La cara bonita
6. Ya lo sé
7. Ni princesa ni esclava
8. No llega el olvido
9. Amaneciste conmigo (Sentirte en mi frío)
10. La escalera
11. La gran señora
12. Amarga Navidad
13. Estaré contigo cuando triste estés (*Before The Next Teardrop Falls*) (versión traducida)

JOYAS PRESTADAS (2011)

1. A cambio de qué
2. A que no le cuentas
3. Así fue
4. Basta ya
5. Como tu mujer
6. Detrás de mi ventana
7. Lo siento mi amor
8. Qué ganas de no verte nunca más
9. Resulta
10. Señora
11. Porque me gusta a morir

LA MISMA GRAN SEÑORA (2012)

1. La misma gran señora
2. Resulta
3. La gran señora
4. Ya lo sé
5. Por qué no le calas
6. Hermano amigo
7. Trono caído
8. Besos y copas
9. Por un amor, cucurrucucú paloma
10. Qué me vas a dar
11. No vas a creer
12. No me pregunten por él
13. Ovarios